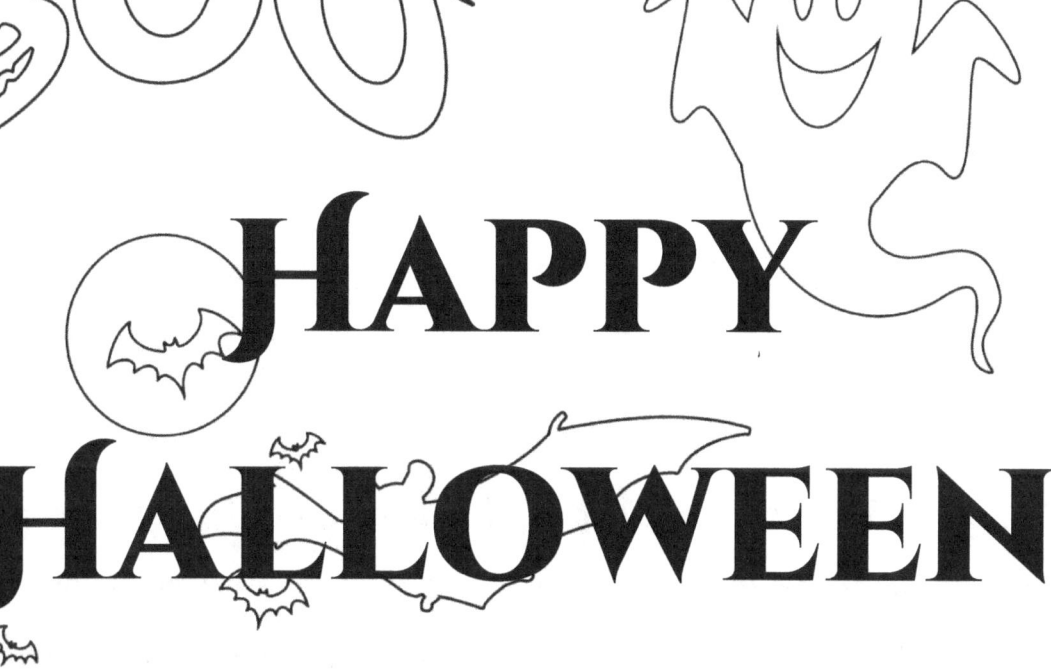

Happy Halloween

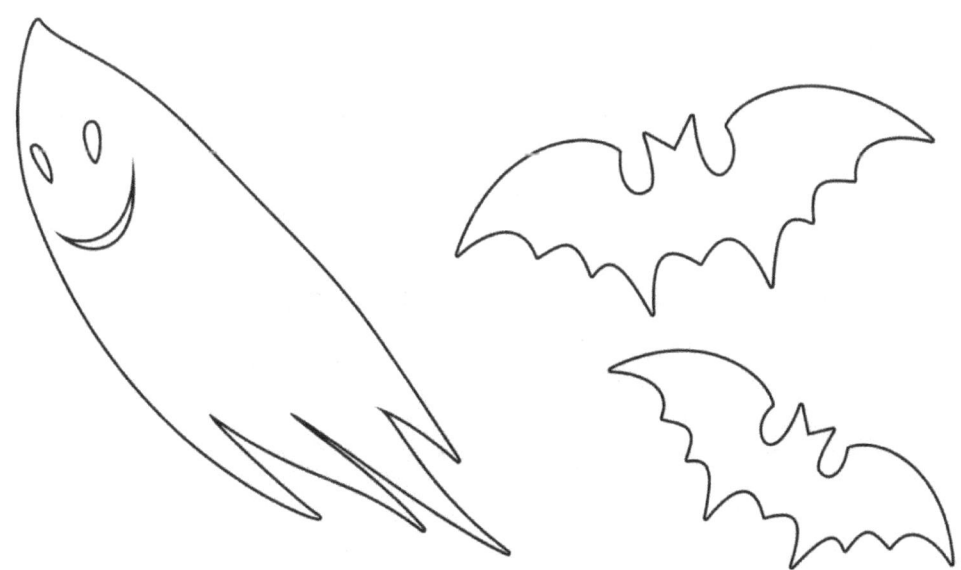

CHARLOTTE GEORGE

Copyright © 2017 Ferneva Books

All rights reserved. No part of this book may be reprinted or reproduced or utilized in any form or by any electronic, mechanical, or other means, now known or hereafter invented, including photocopying and recording, or in information storage or retrieval systems, without permission in writing from the author.

ISBN-13: 978-1977805911
ISBN-10: 1977805914

Getting Started

This is a Halloween edition of my Adult Colouring series and I hope you enjoy colouring them as much as I have loved creating them.

There are many different levels of colouring for you to enjoy, some simpler ones to ease beginners in, some more challenging ones and then there are some really detailed ones that will take just a little longer. The choice is yours depending on your mood, colouring expertise level or your time constraints. But whatever level you decide to do, just enjoy your time colouring. There are some mini samples at the back of the book to practice your colour choices on if you like.

Here's what to do to get started:

- Pick somewhere quiet to colour and switch off your phone, tablet, computer, or any other distracting media.
- Try to have a flat surface to work on but your lap is fine if you find that more relaxing.
- Pick a Ghoul or Haunted House etc. From the 40 original designs in this book and begin colouring. Let your imagination run away with you and begin to feel the pleasure of having some precious non-thinking time.
- You will be pleasantly surprised at how addictive colouring becomes and how much enjoyment there is in something this simple.

So pick up your pens and enjoy some colouring therapy.

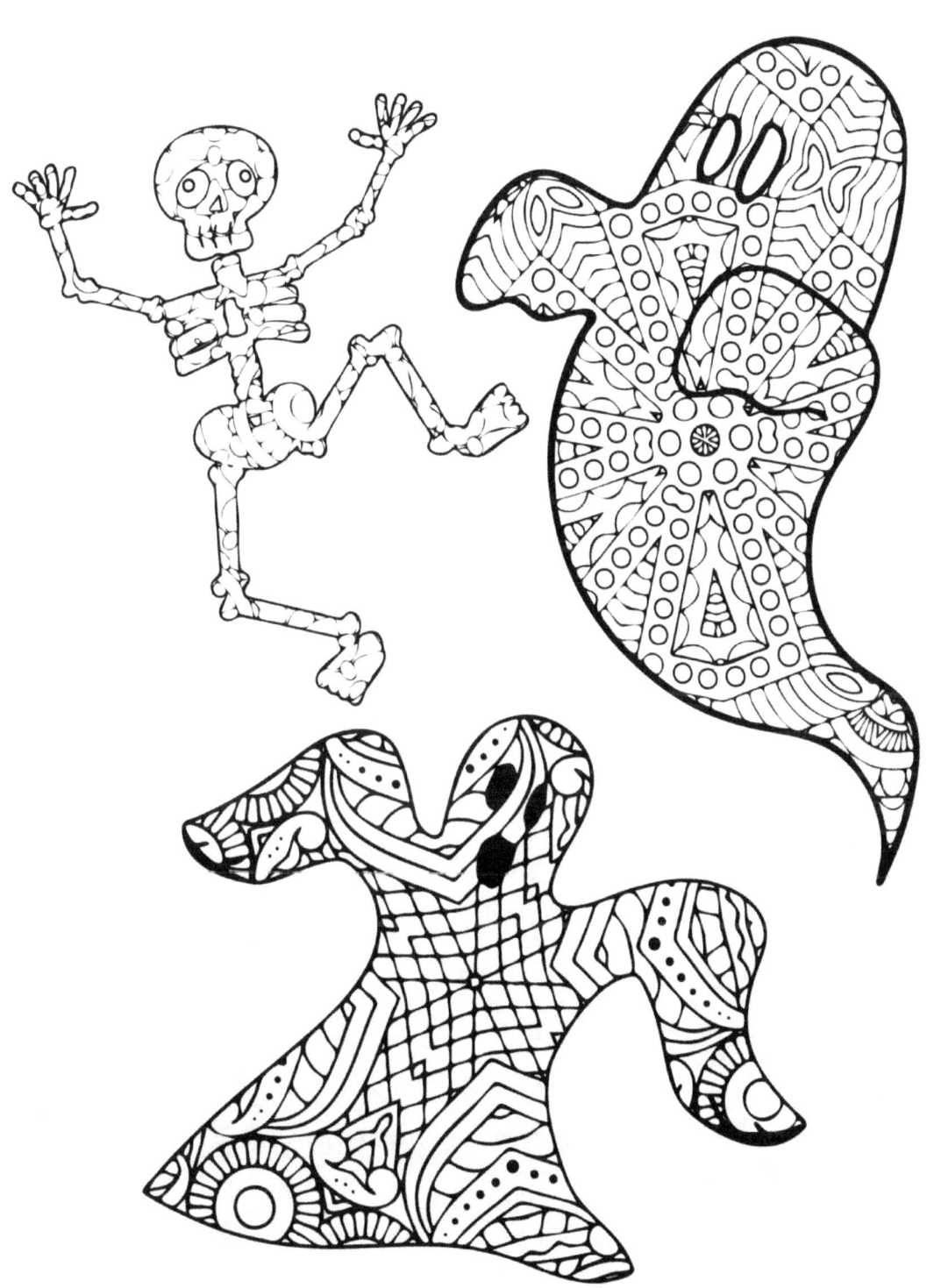

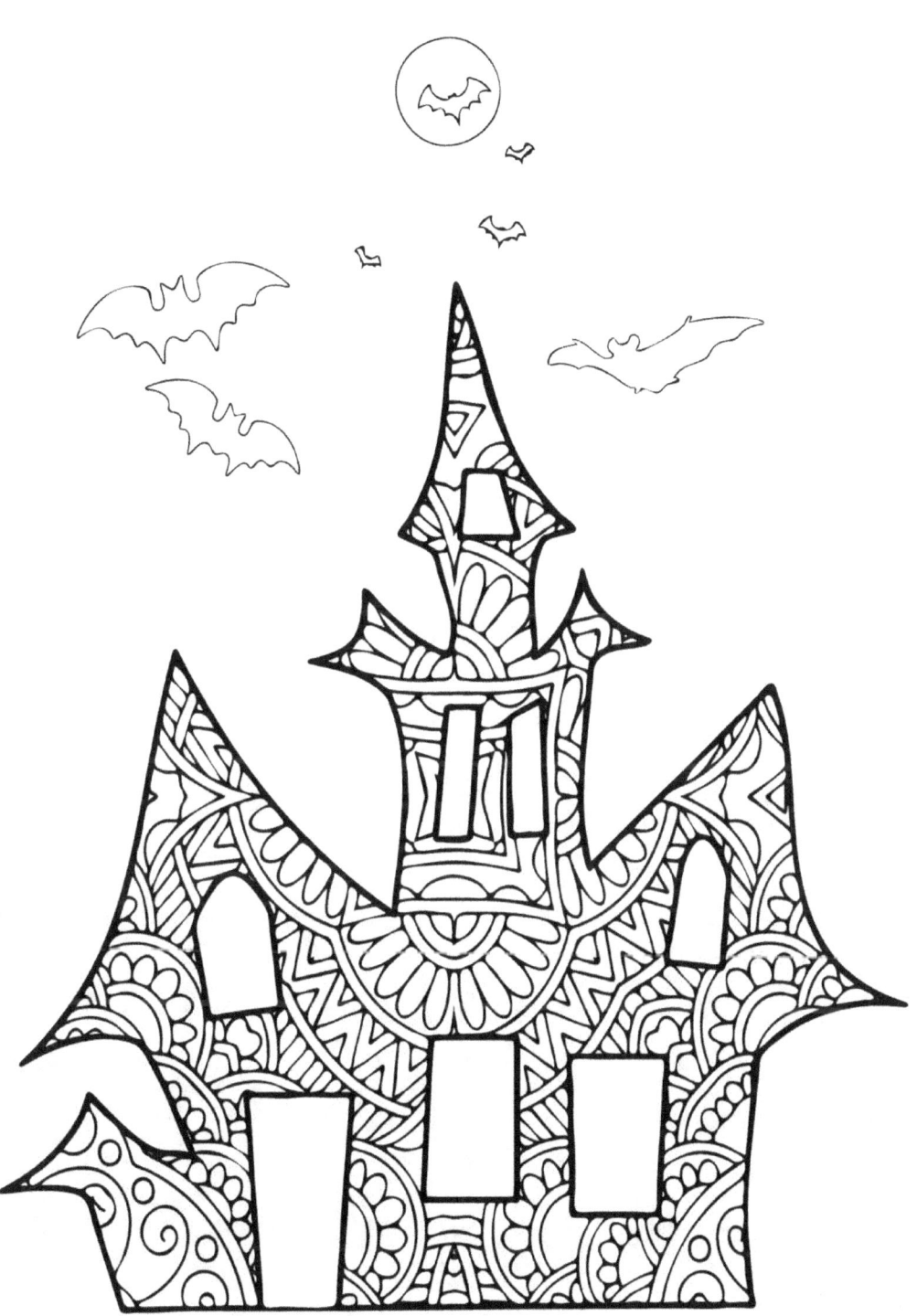

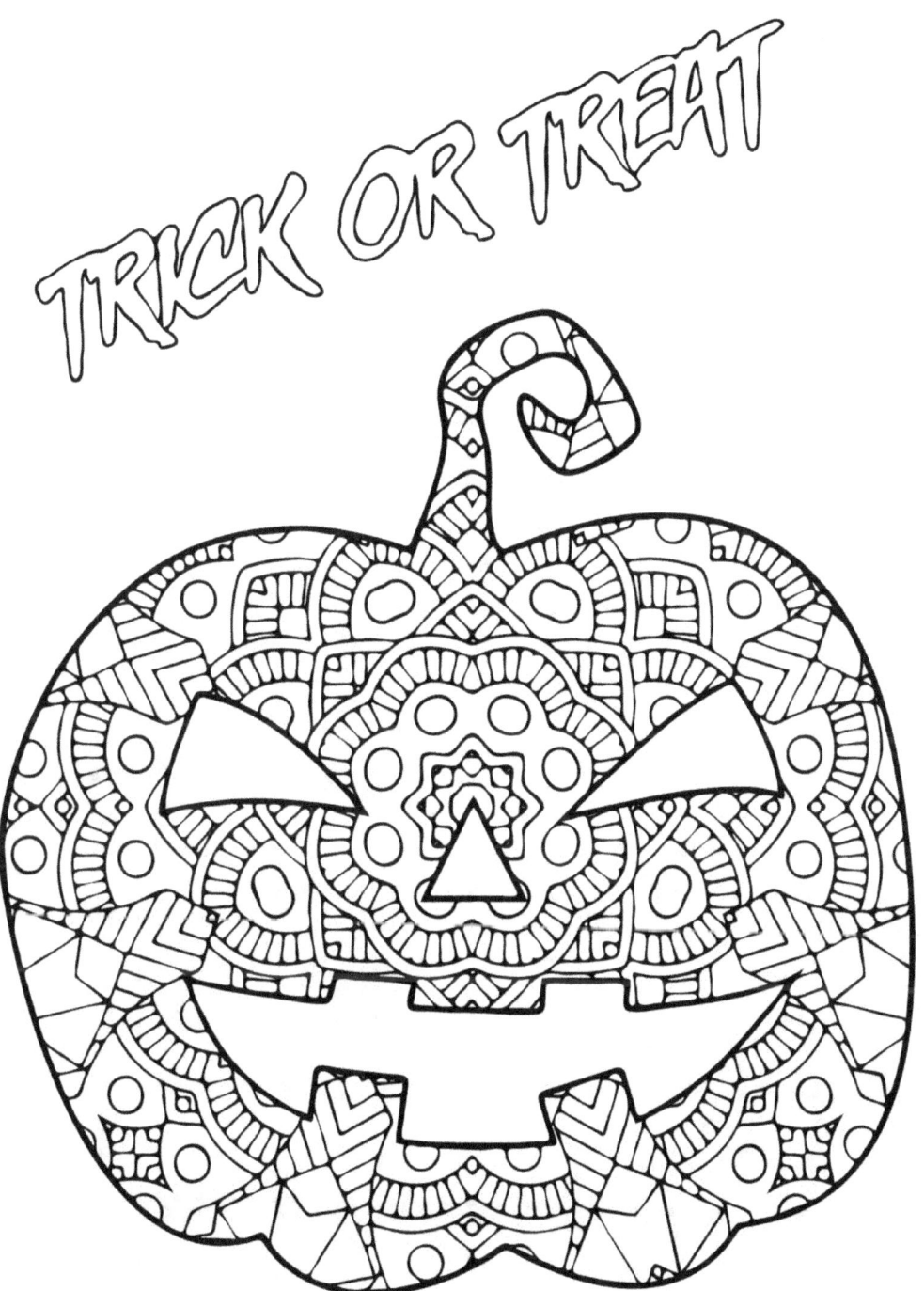

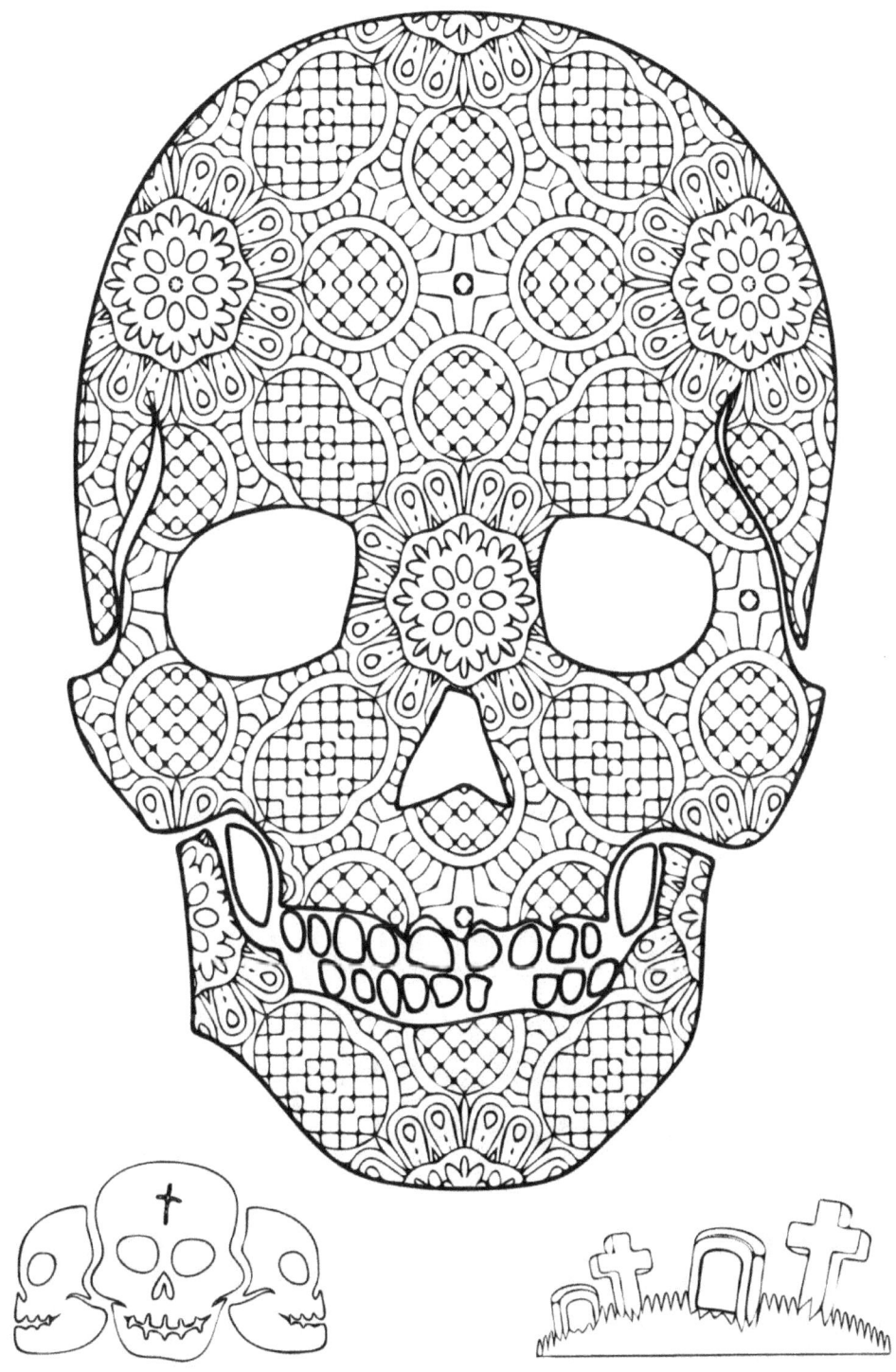

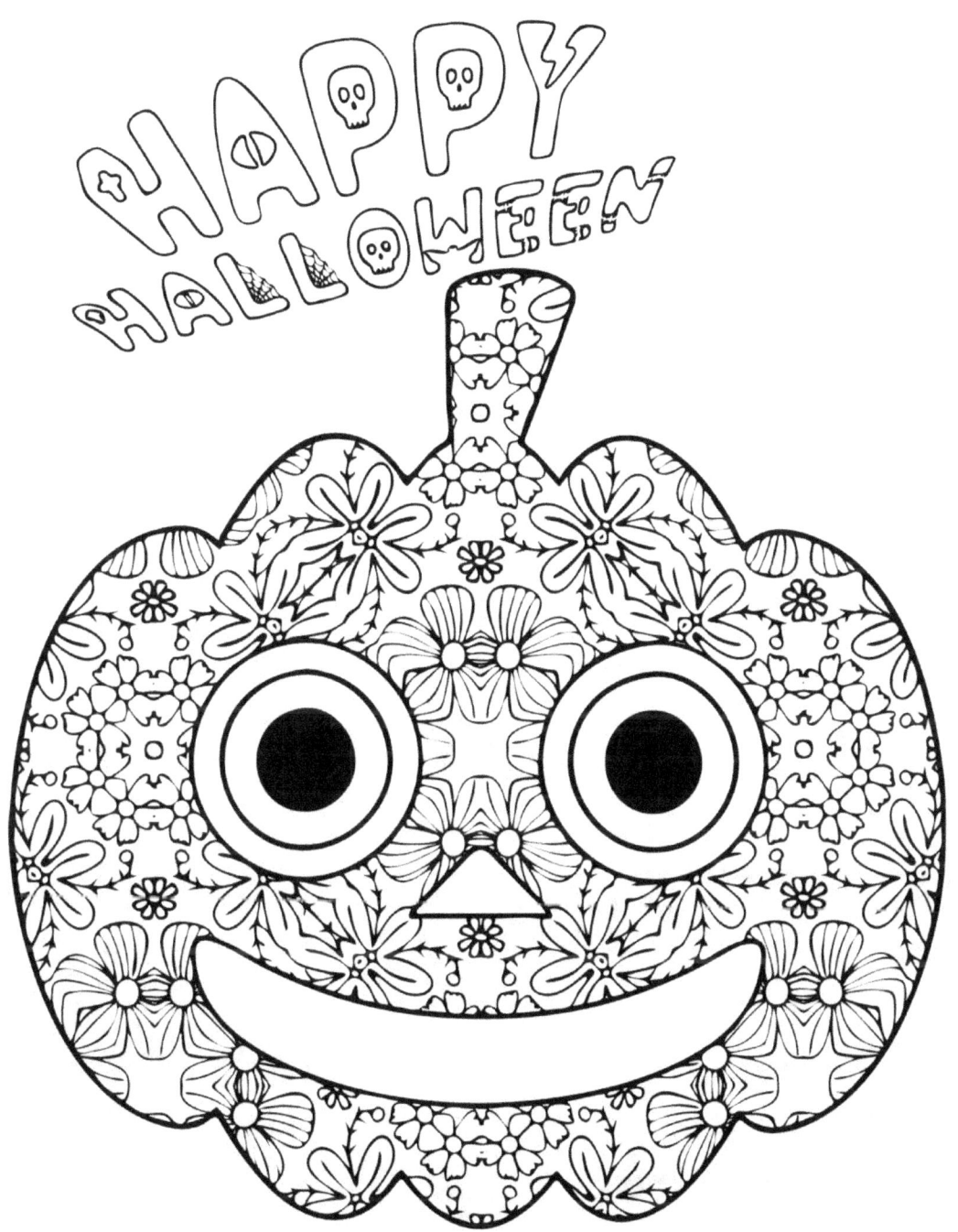

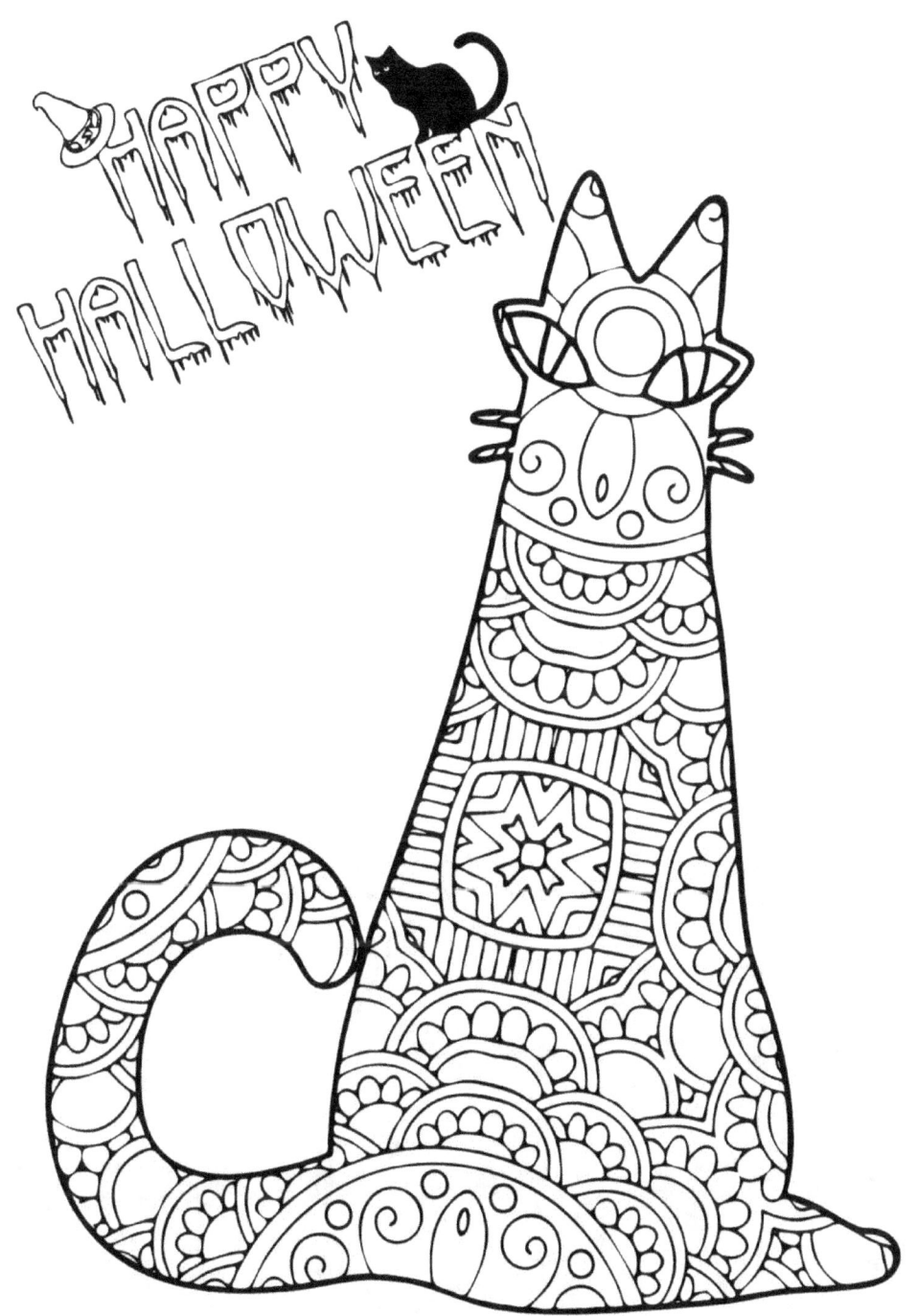

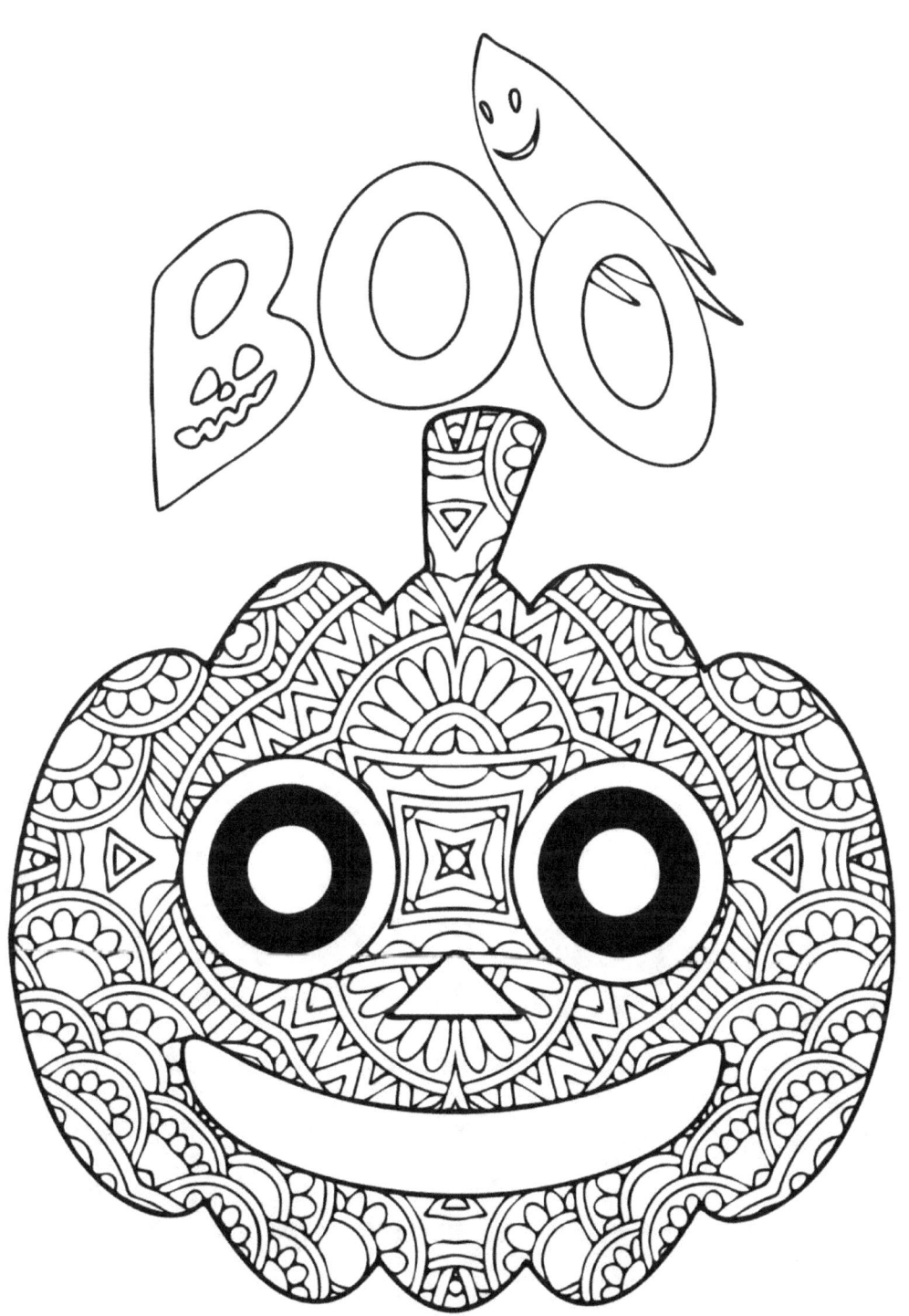

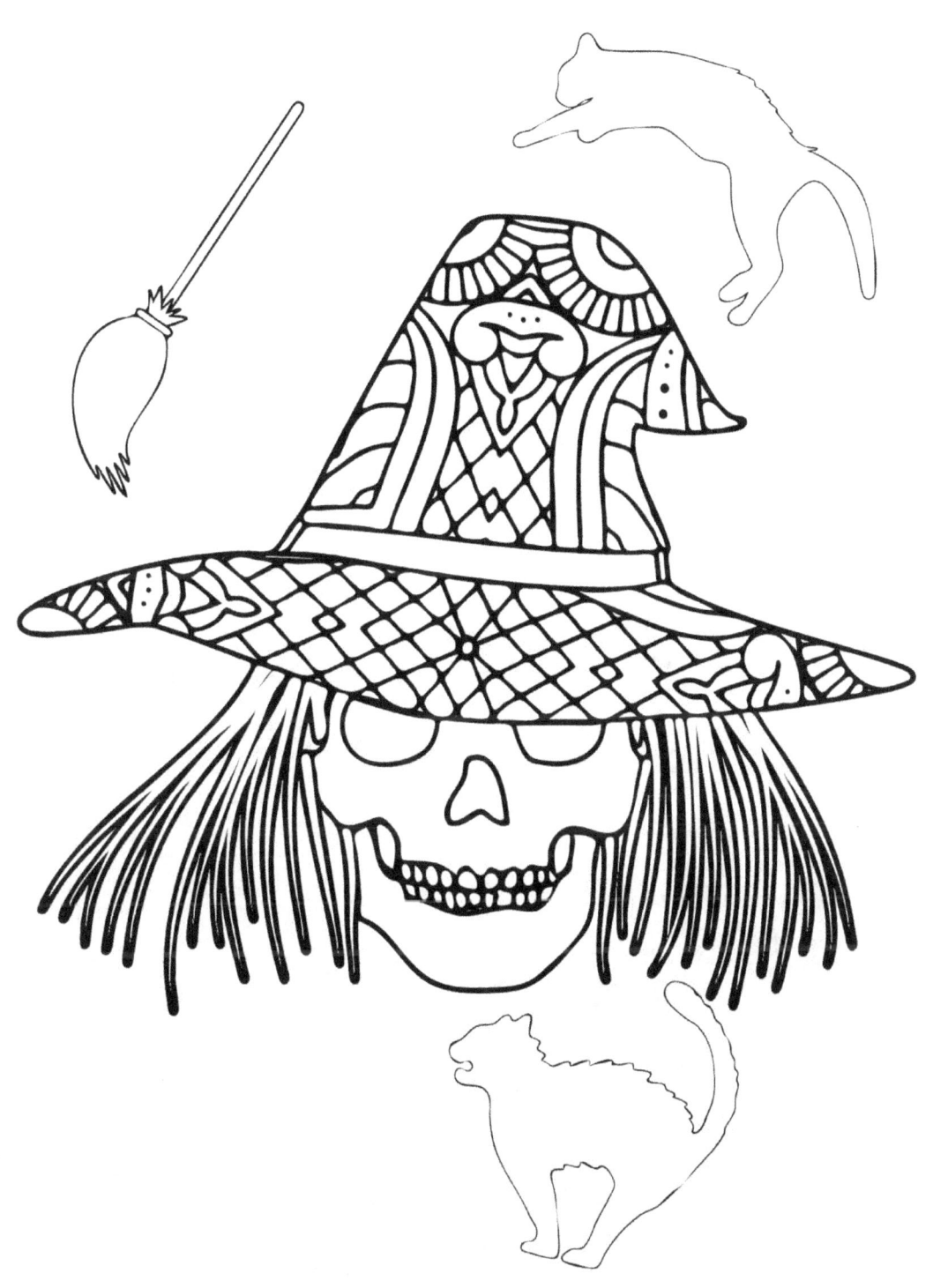

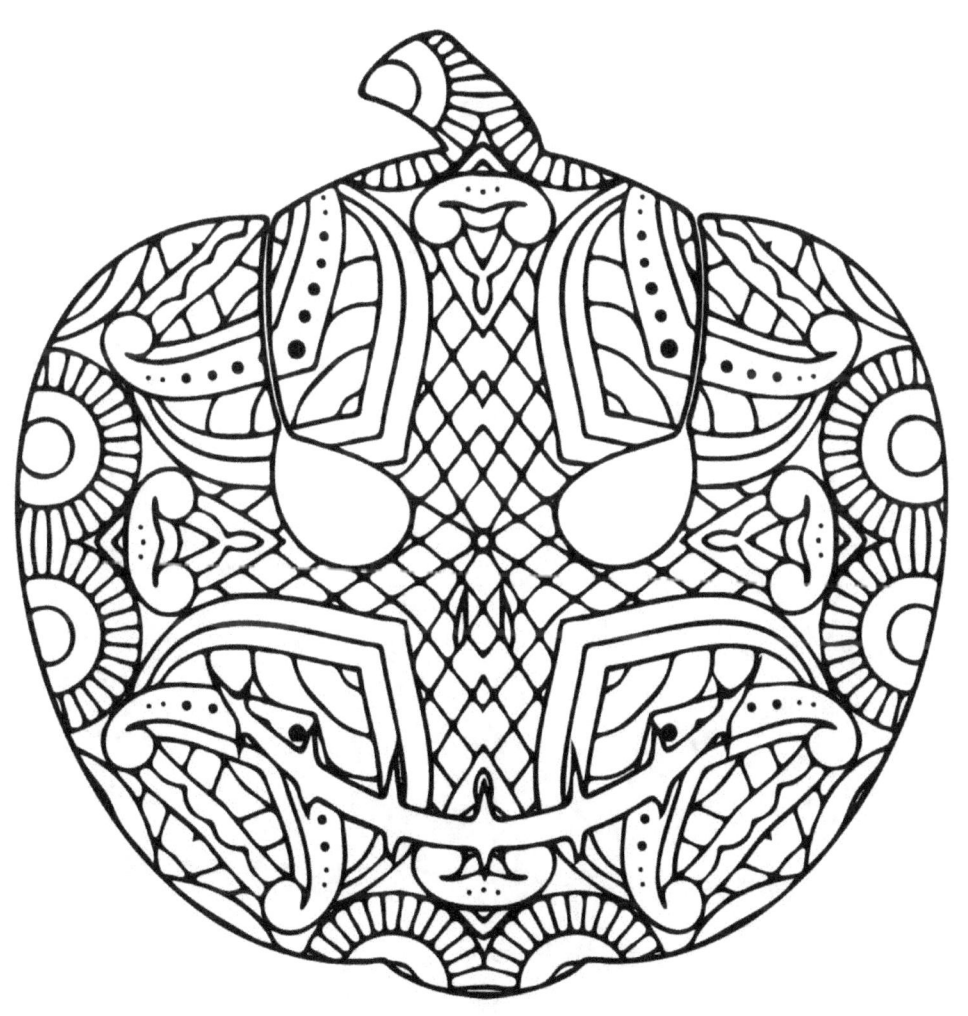

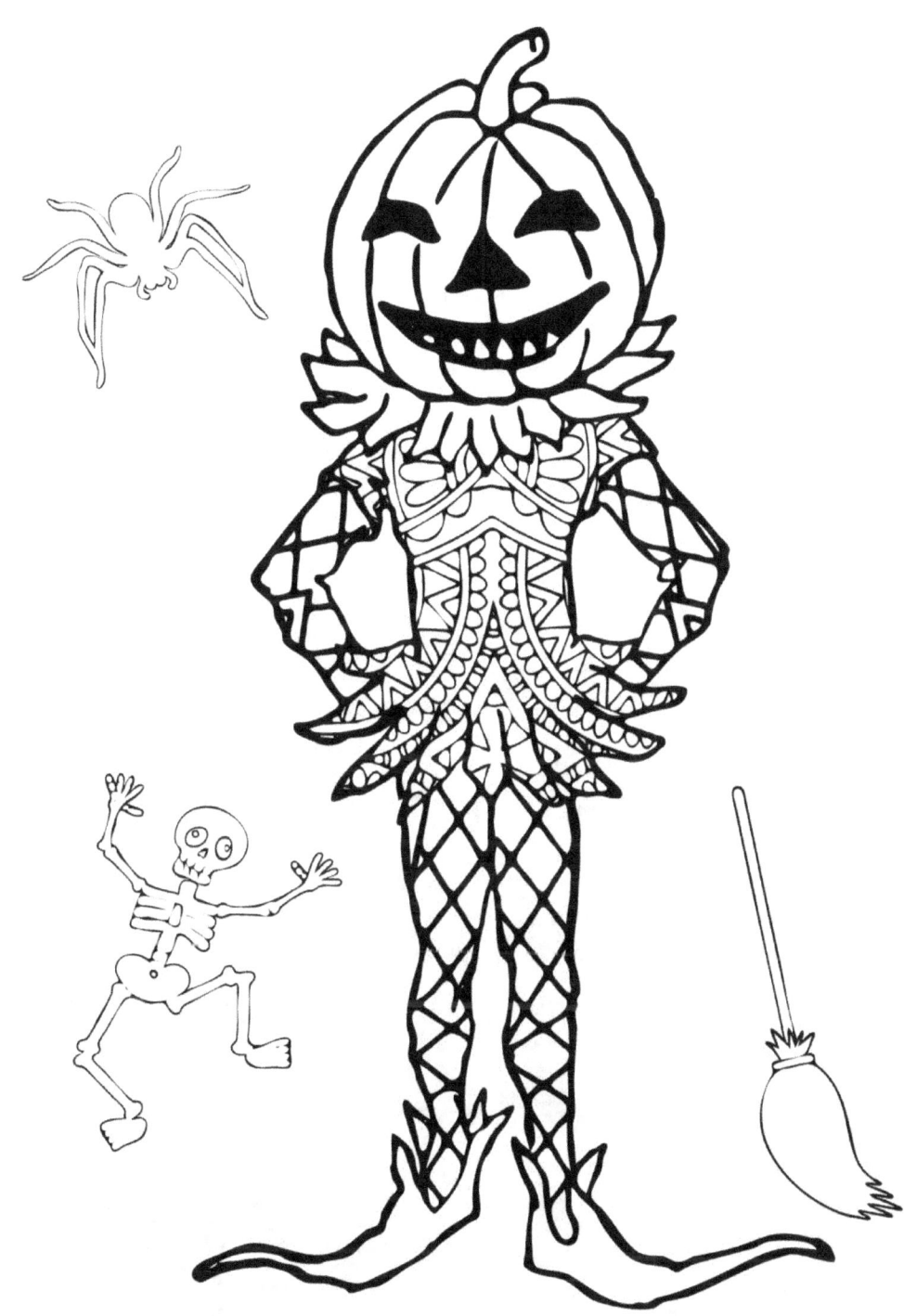

I HATE THE DARK

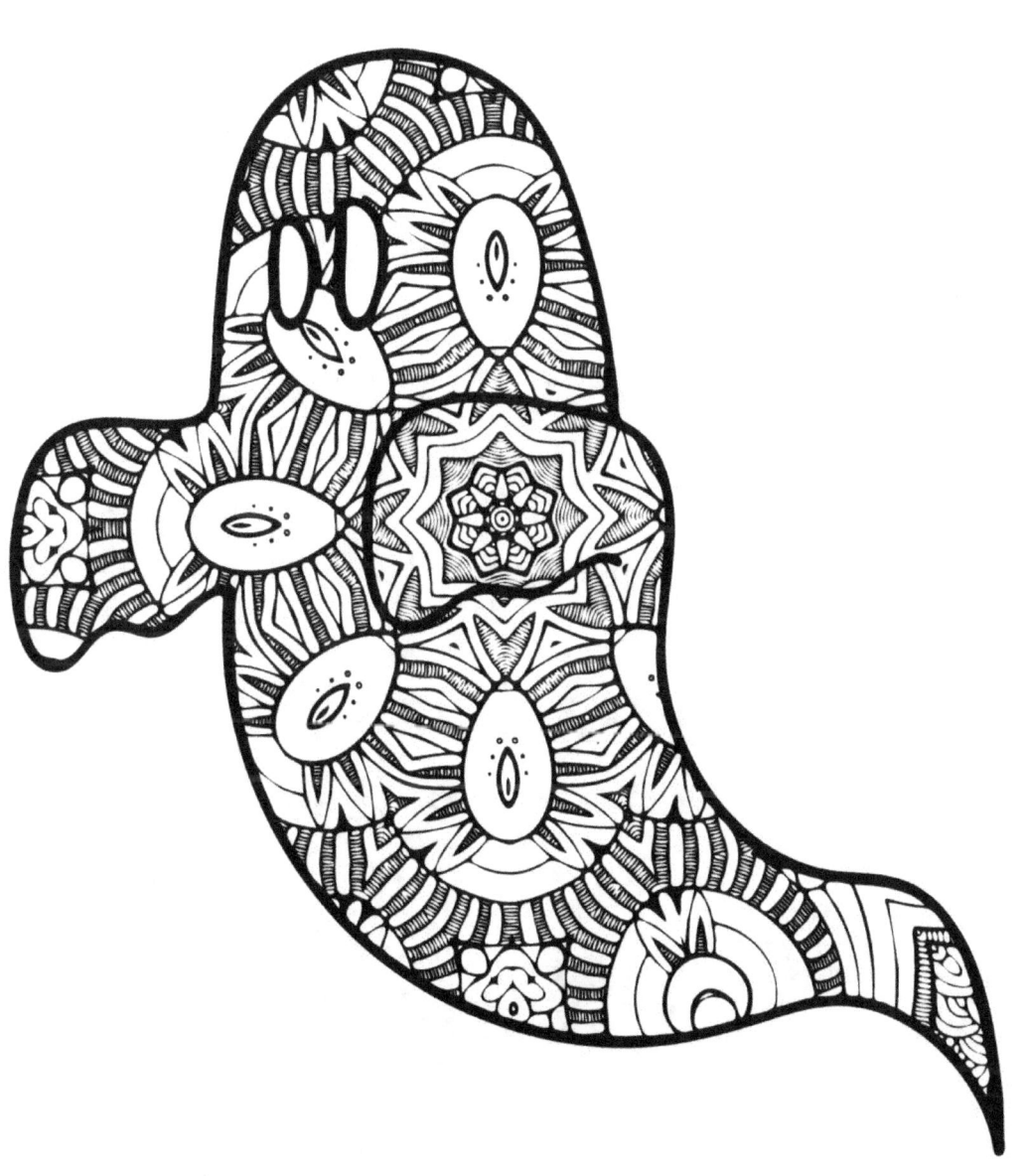

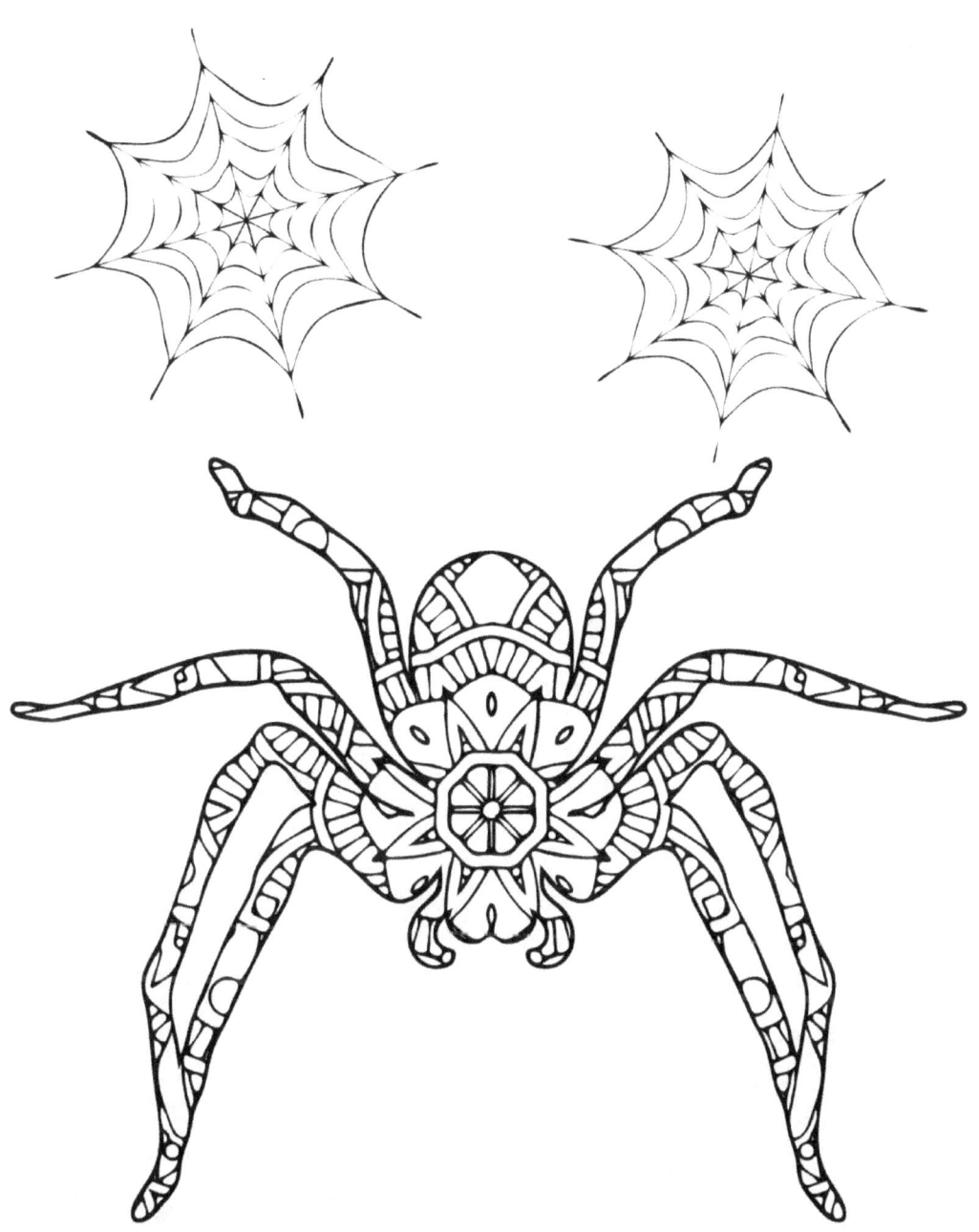

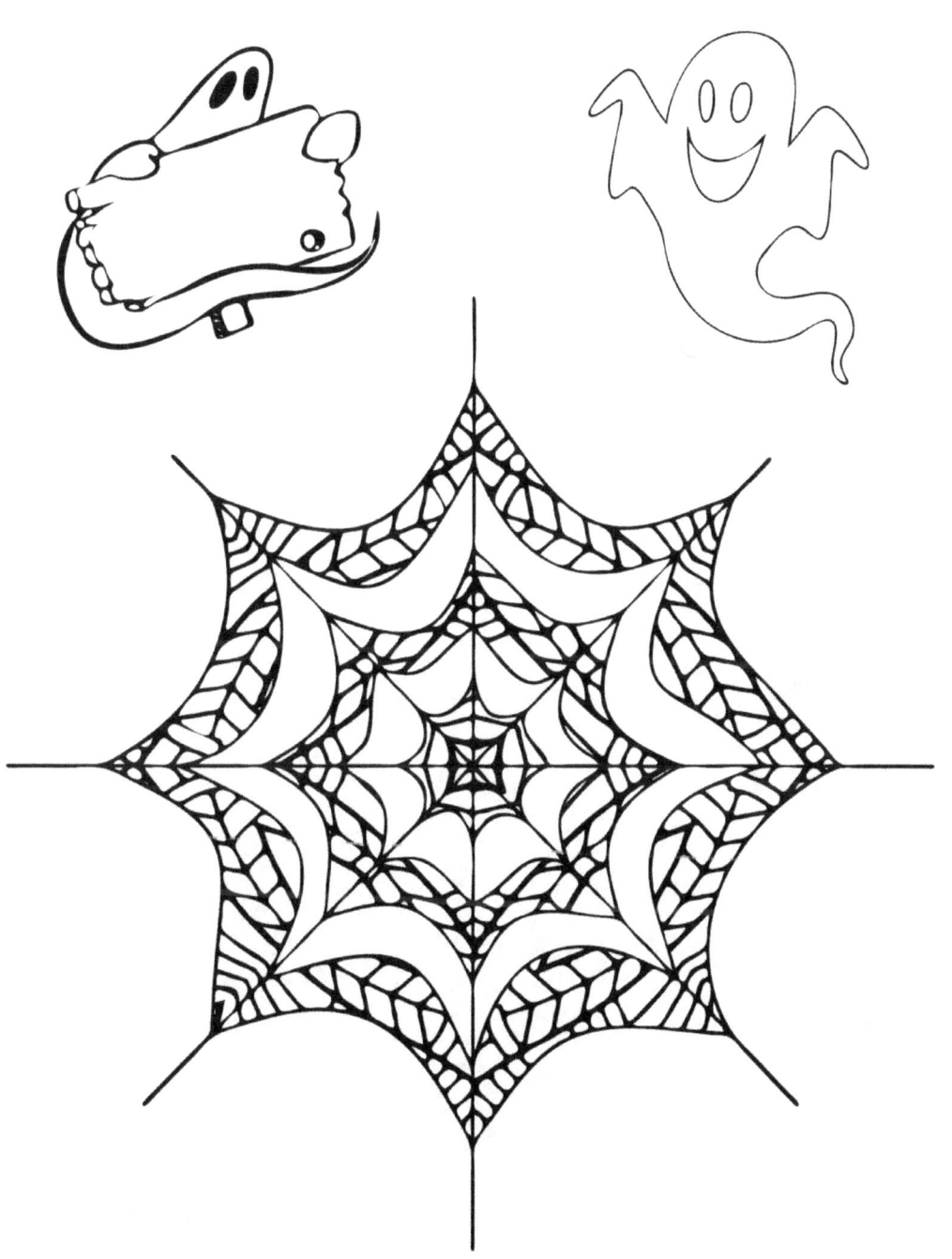

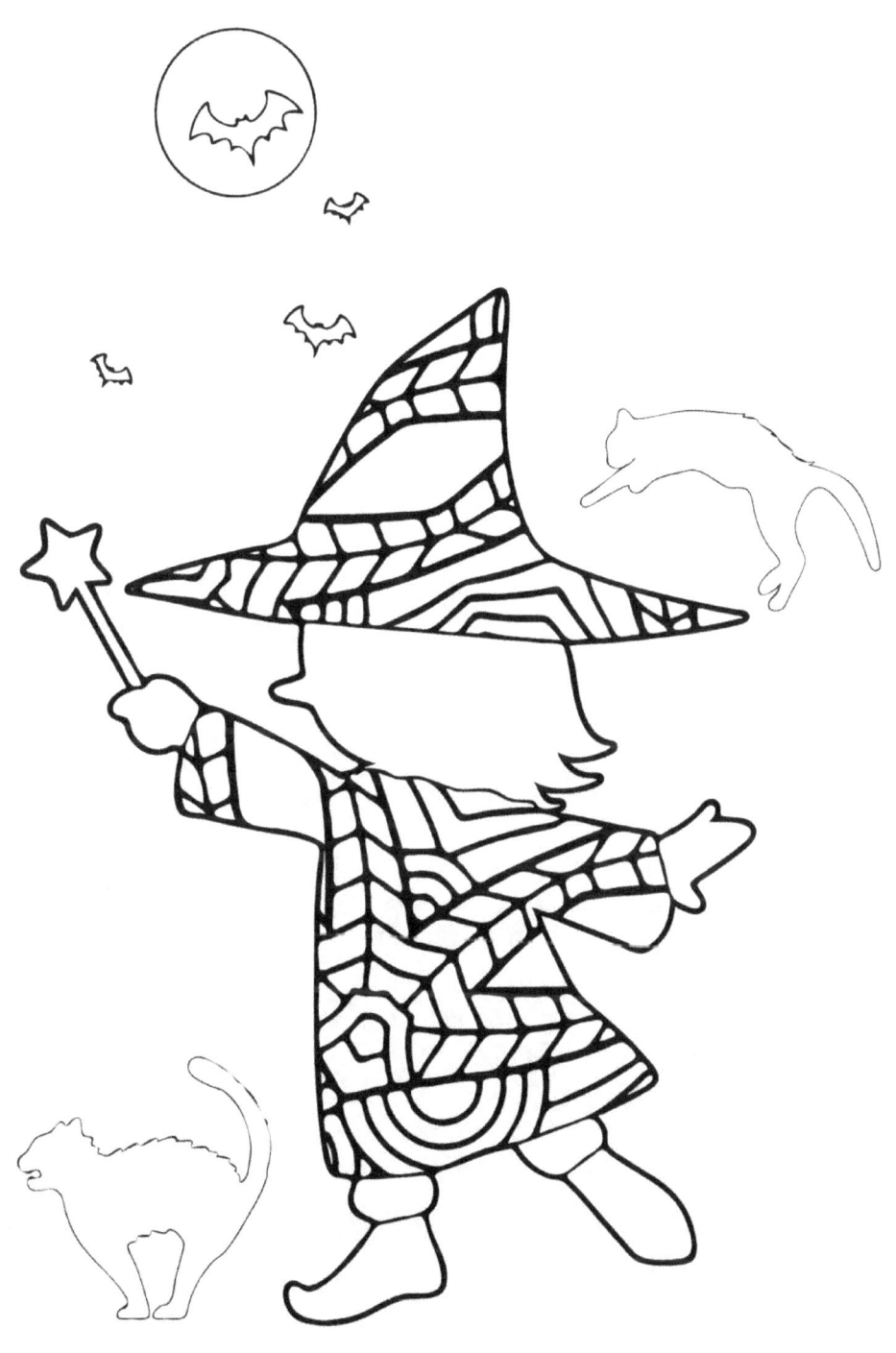

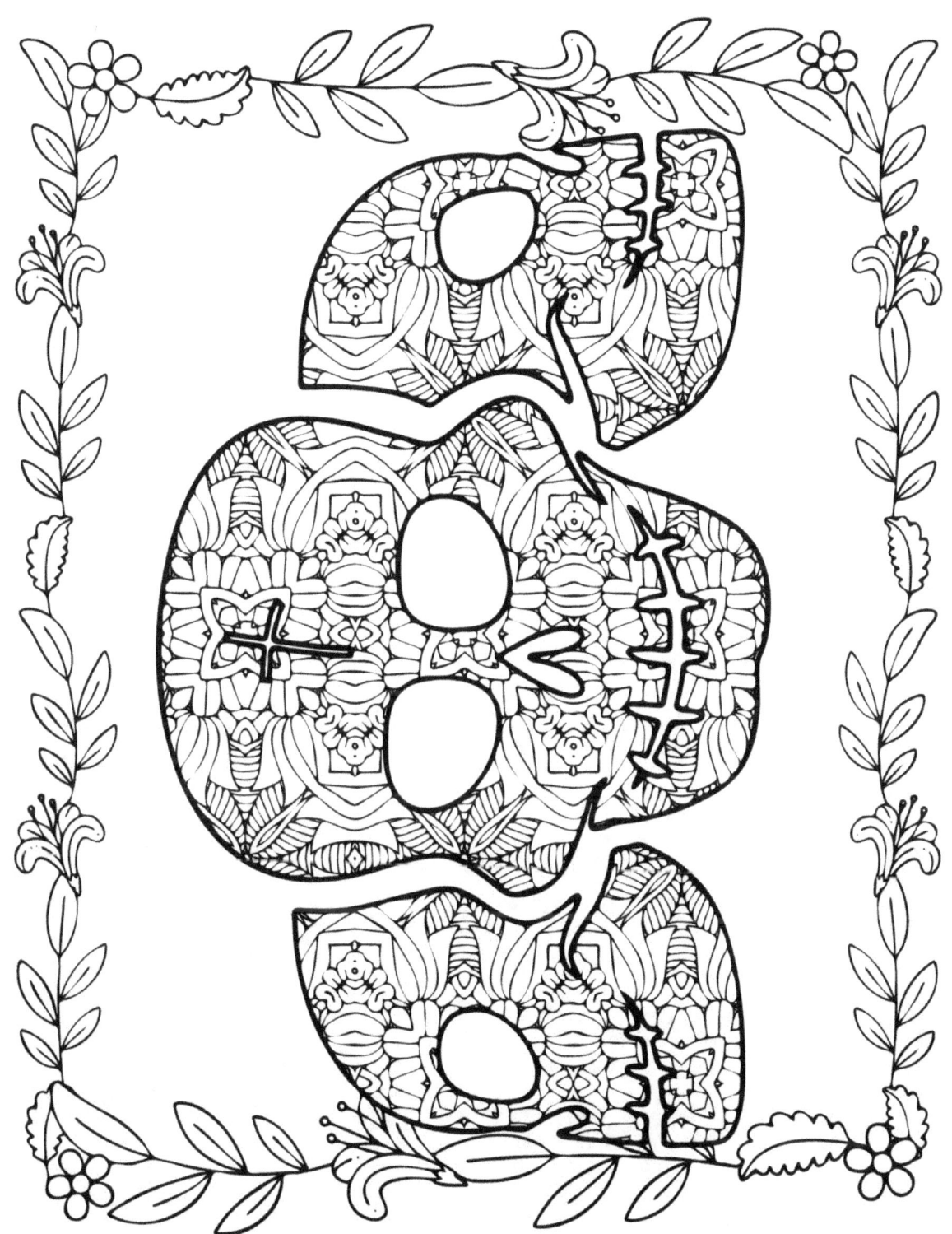

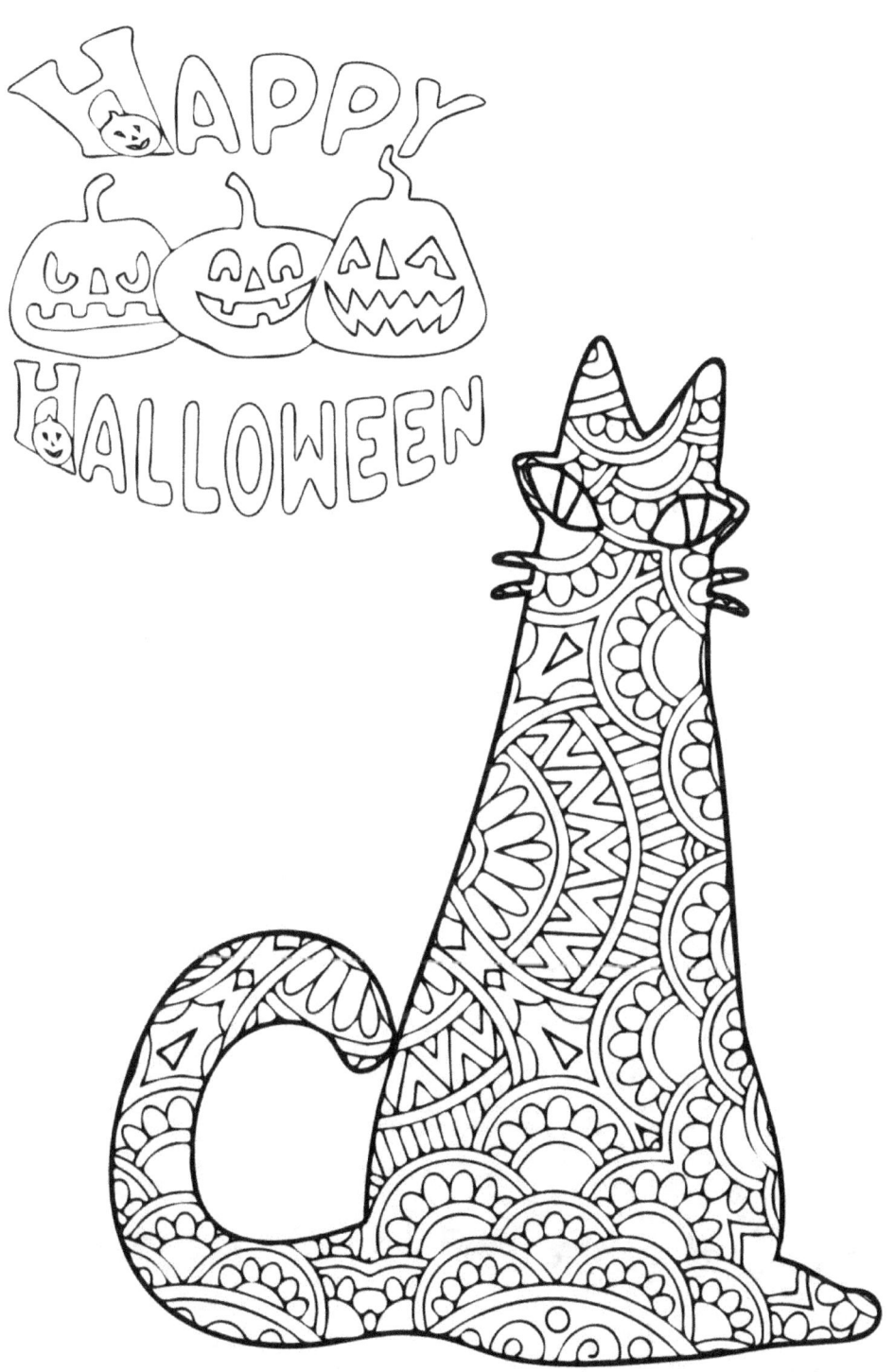

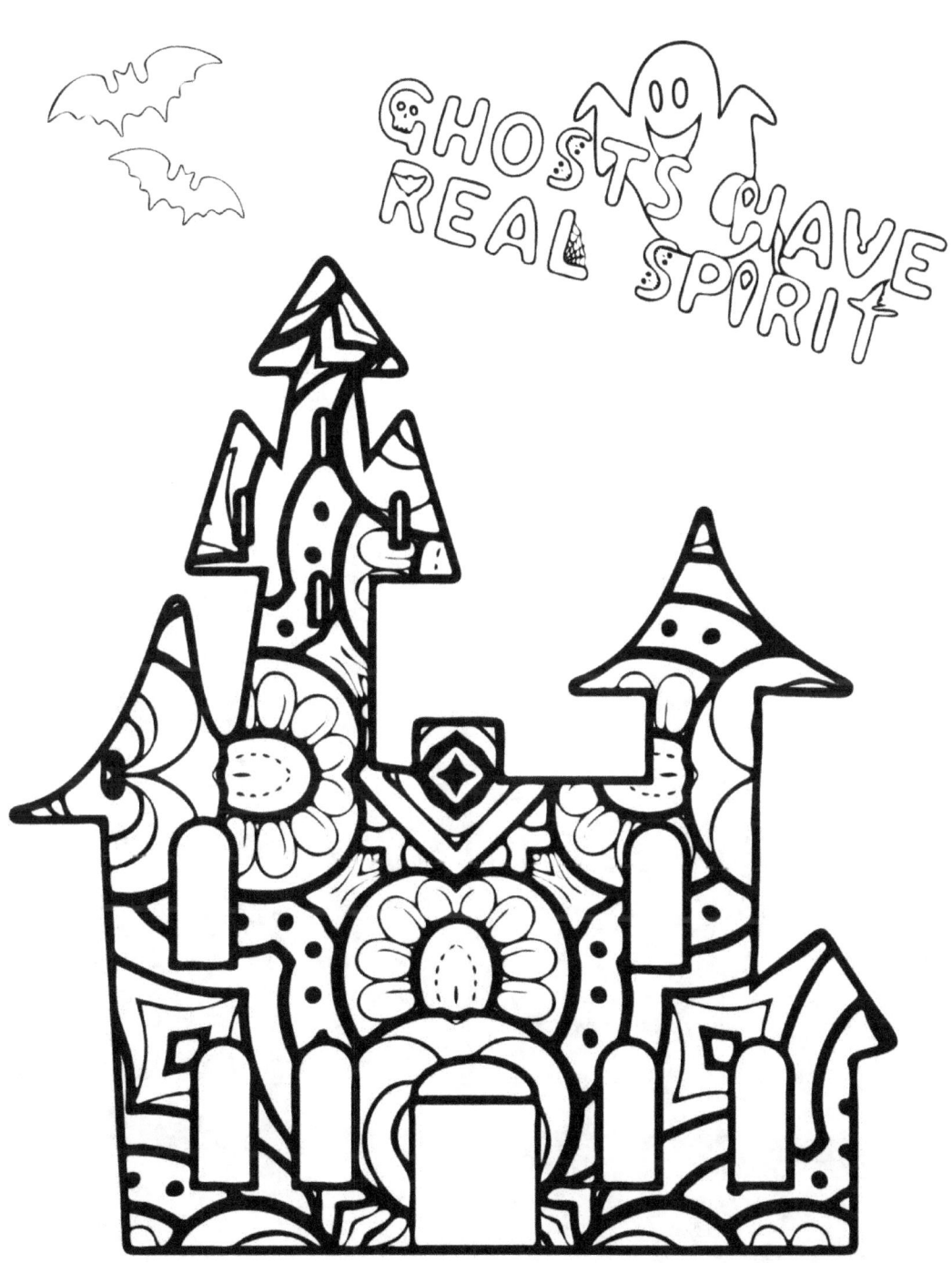

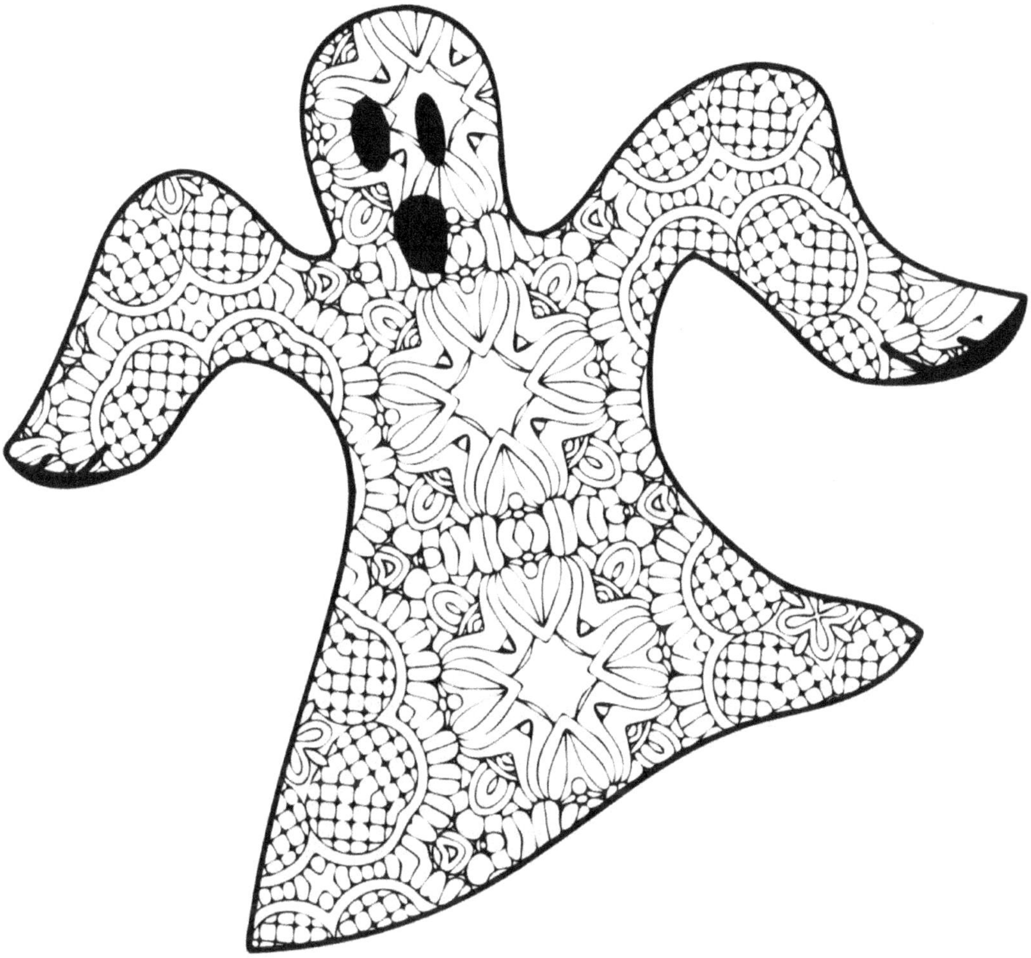

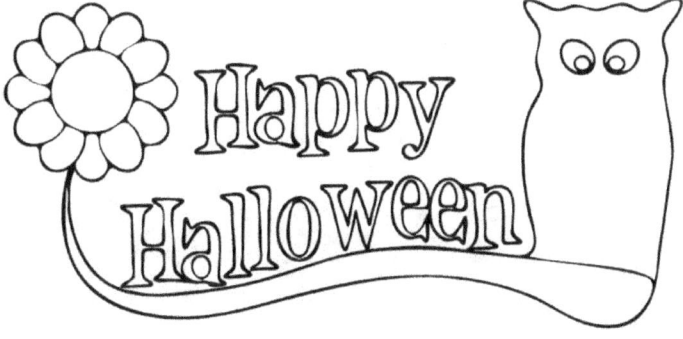

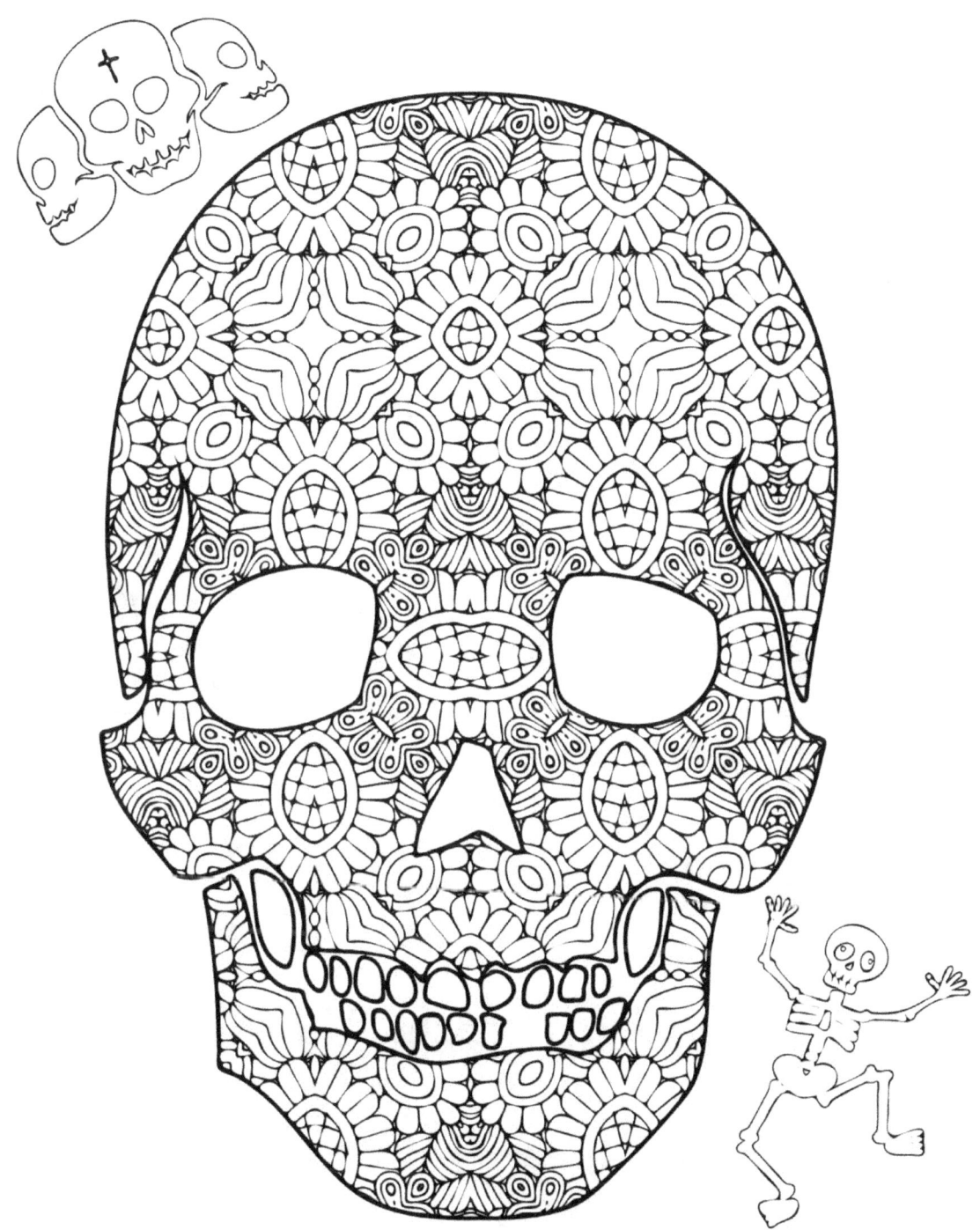

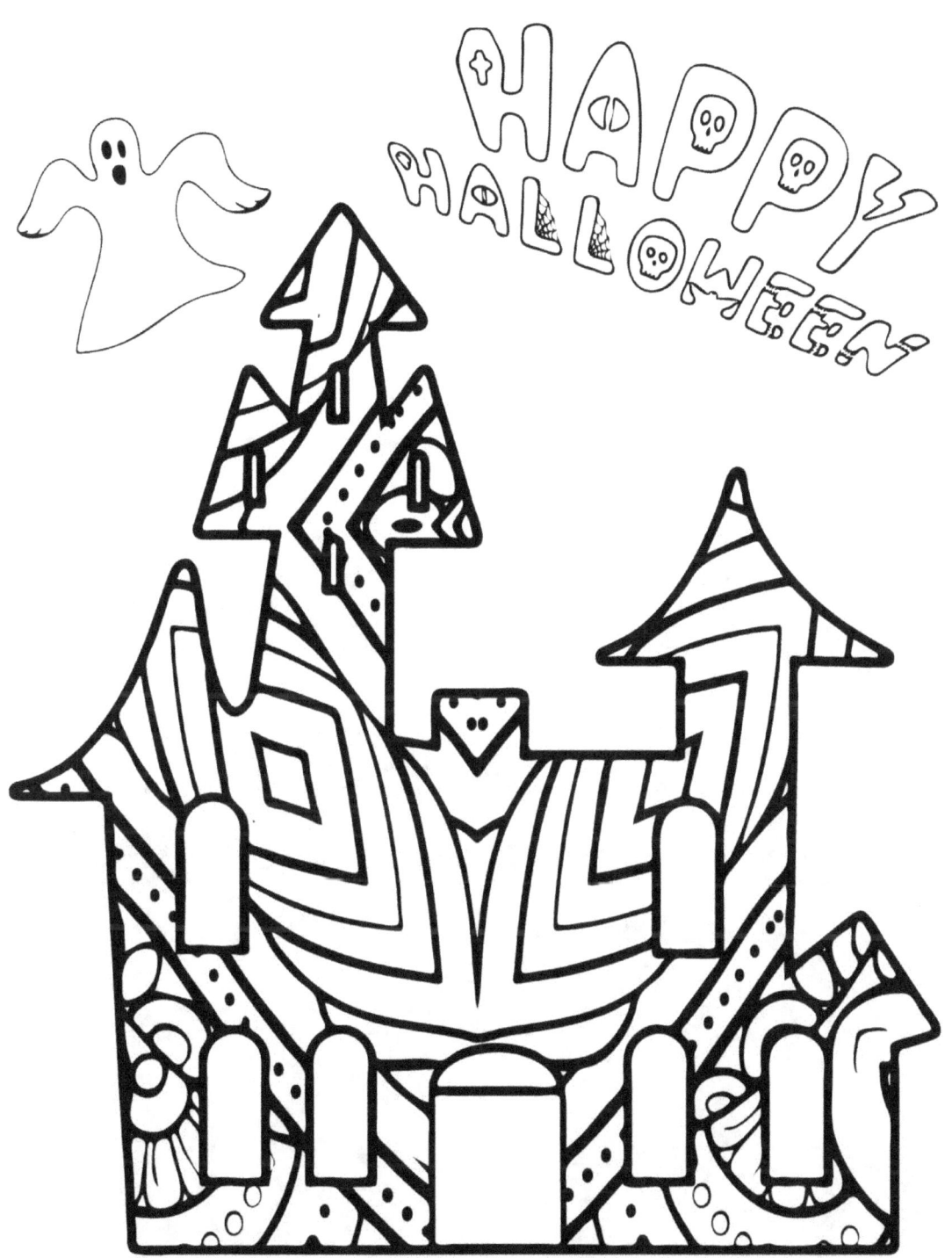

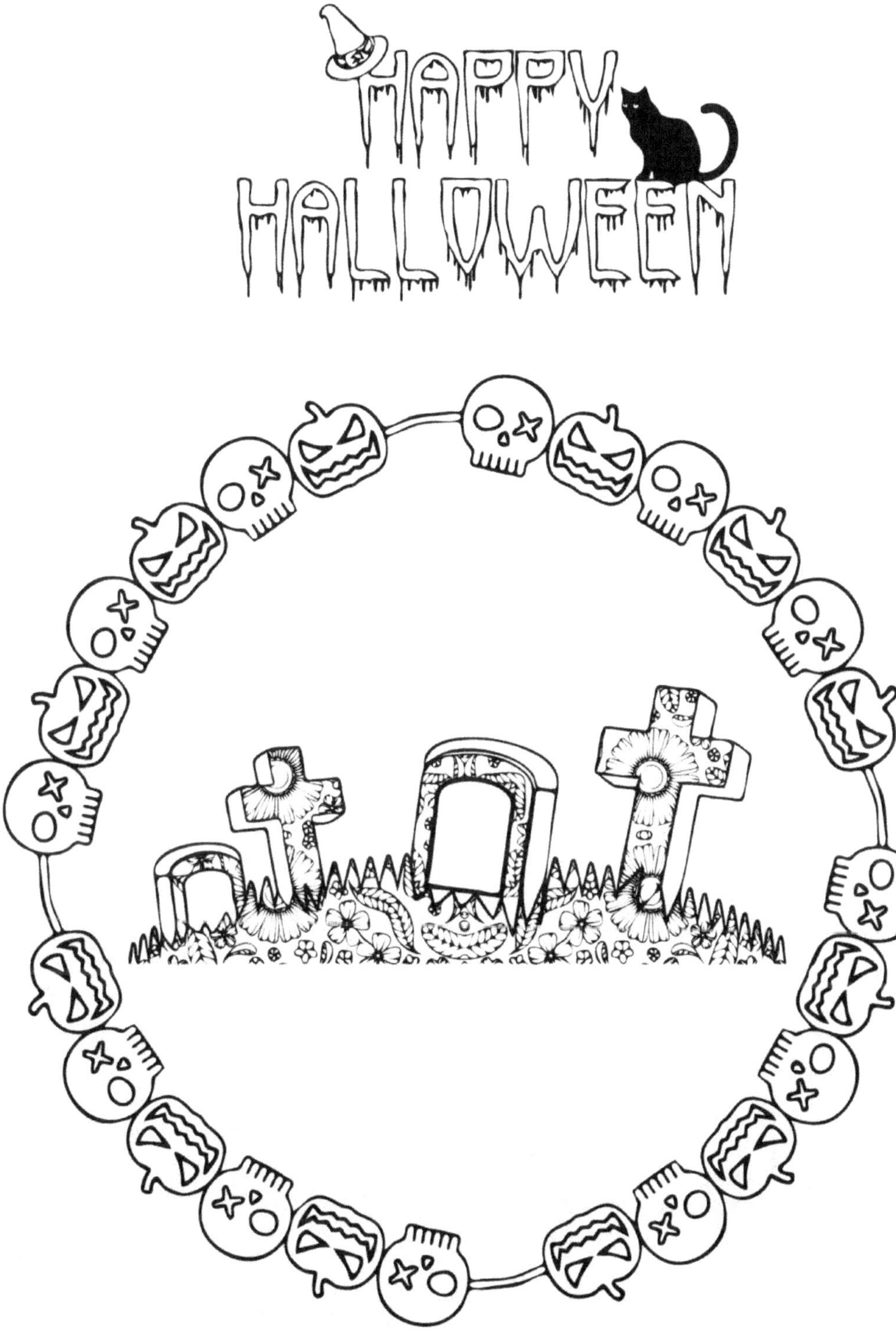

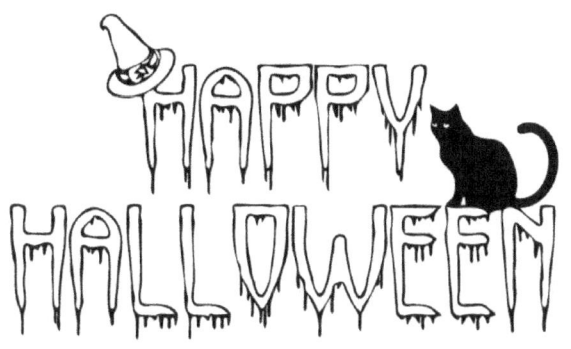

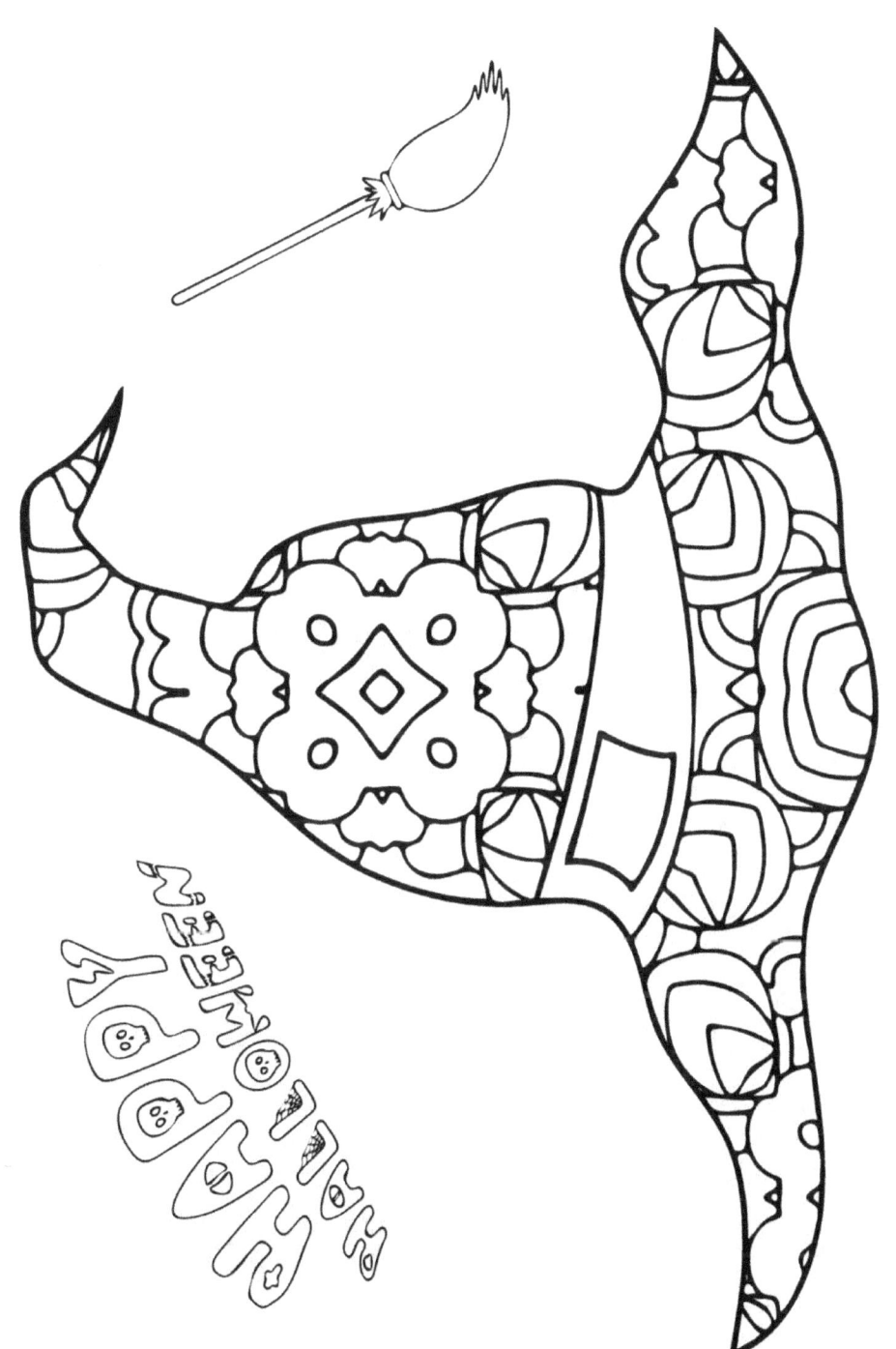

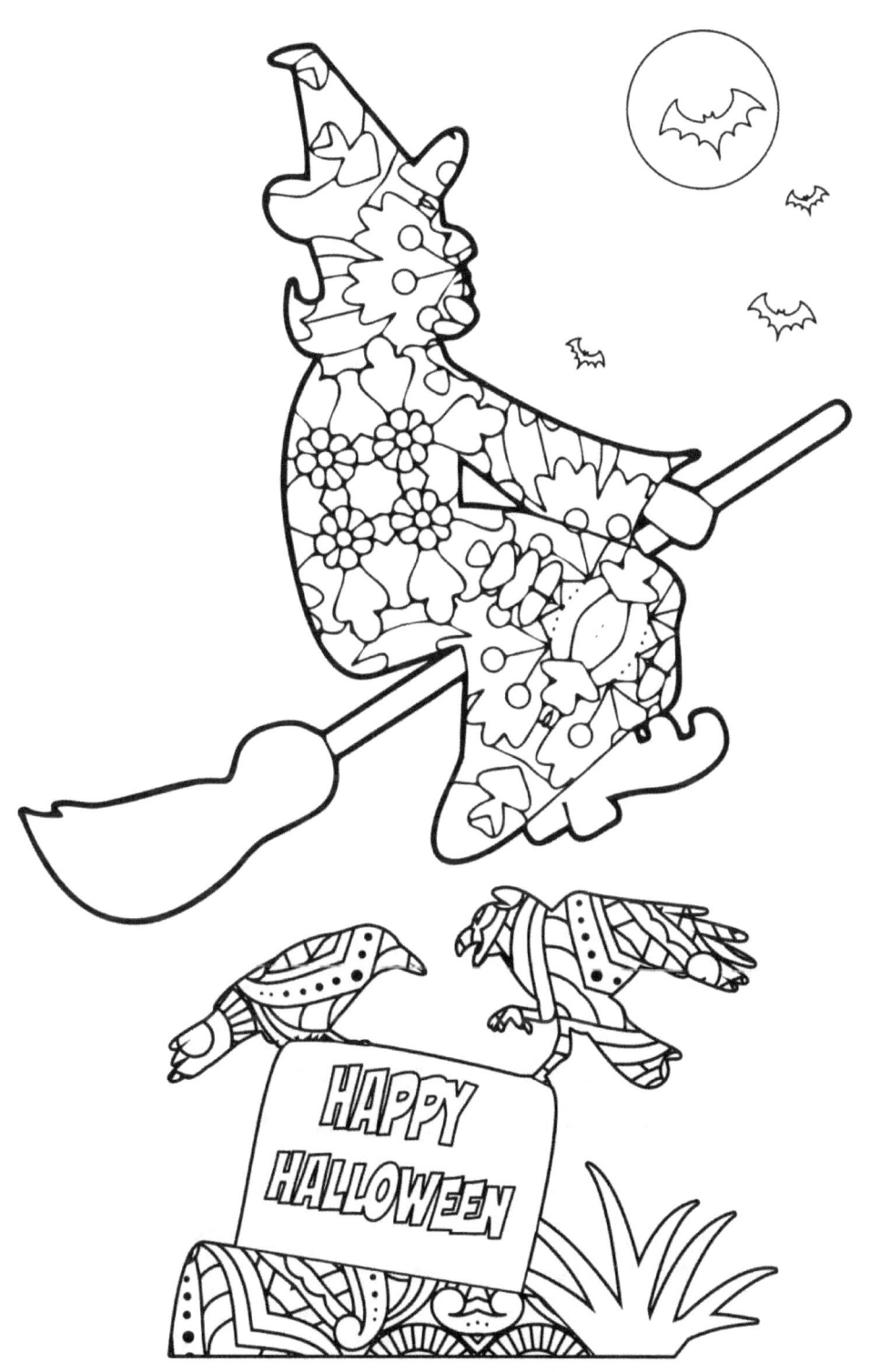

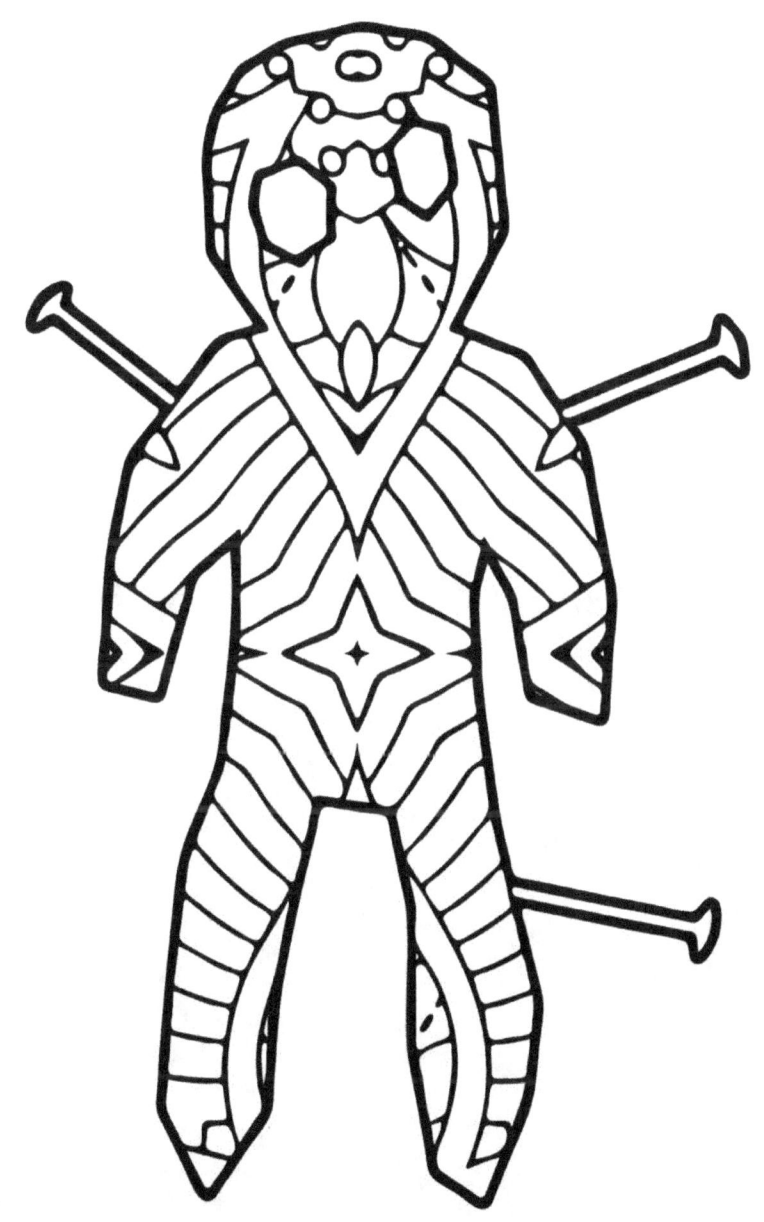

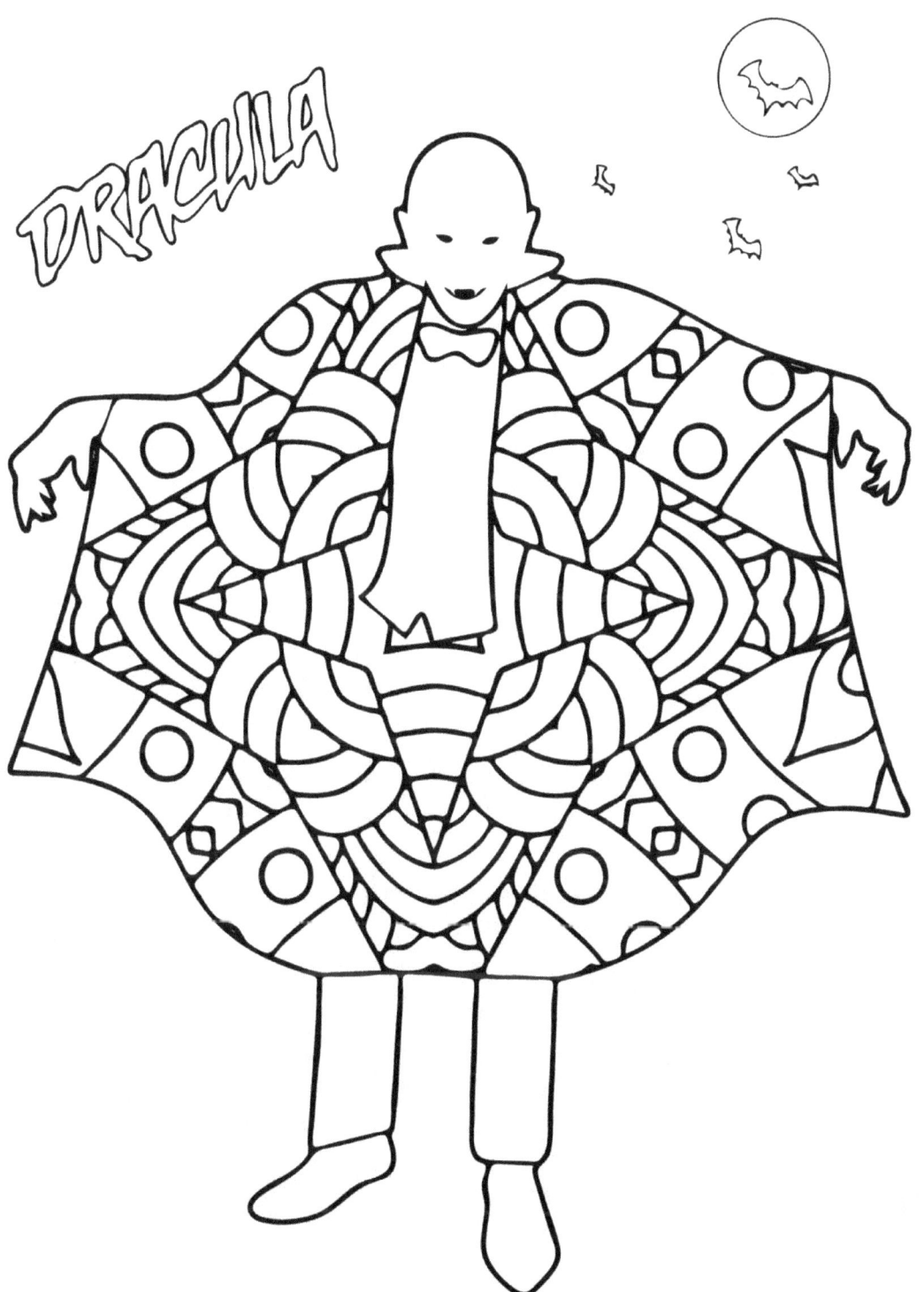

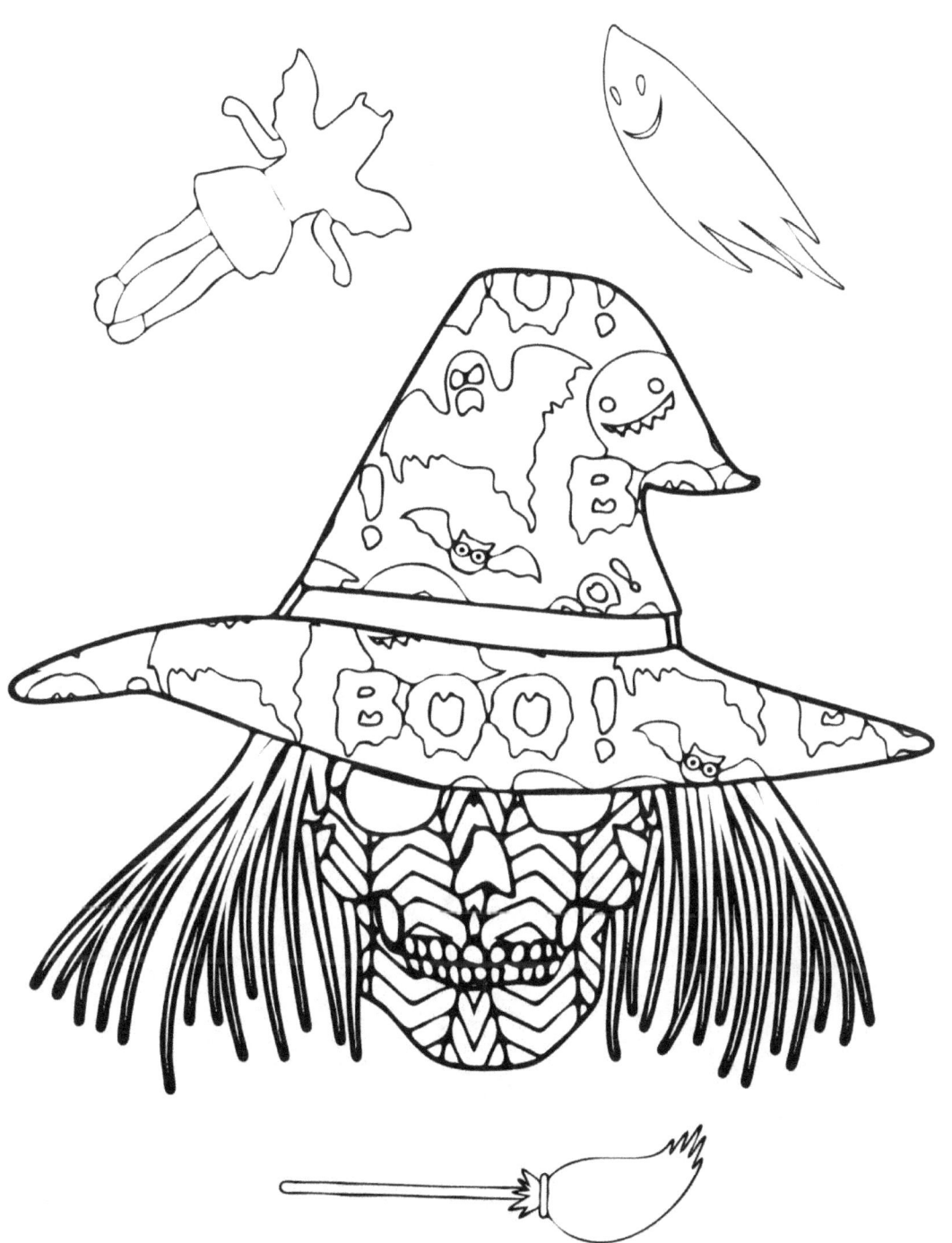

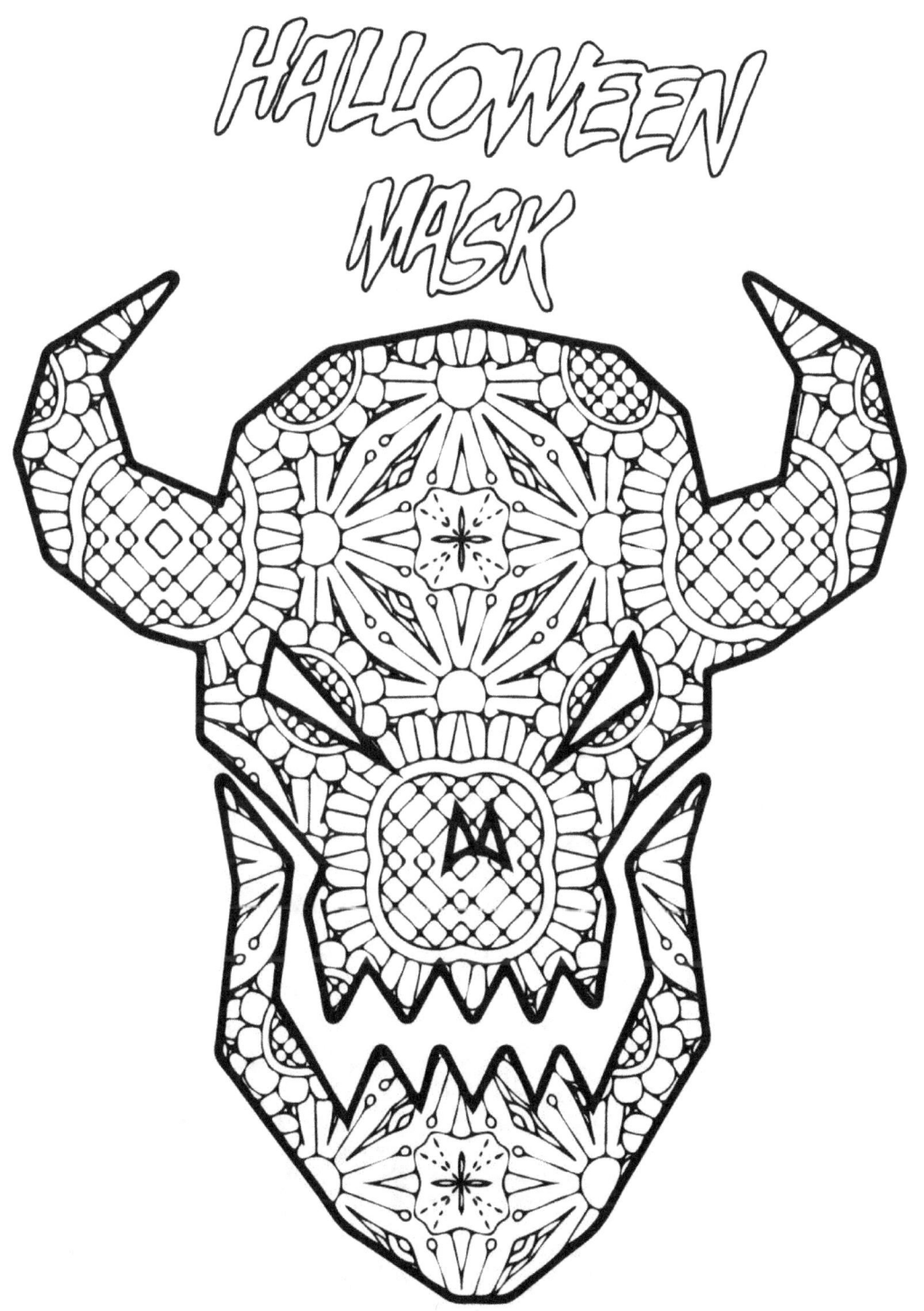

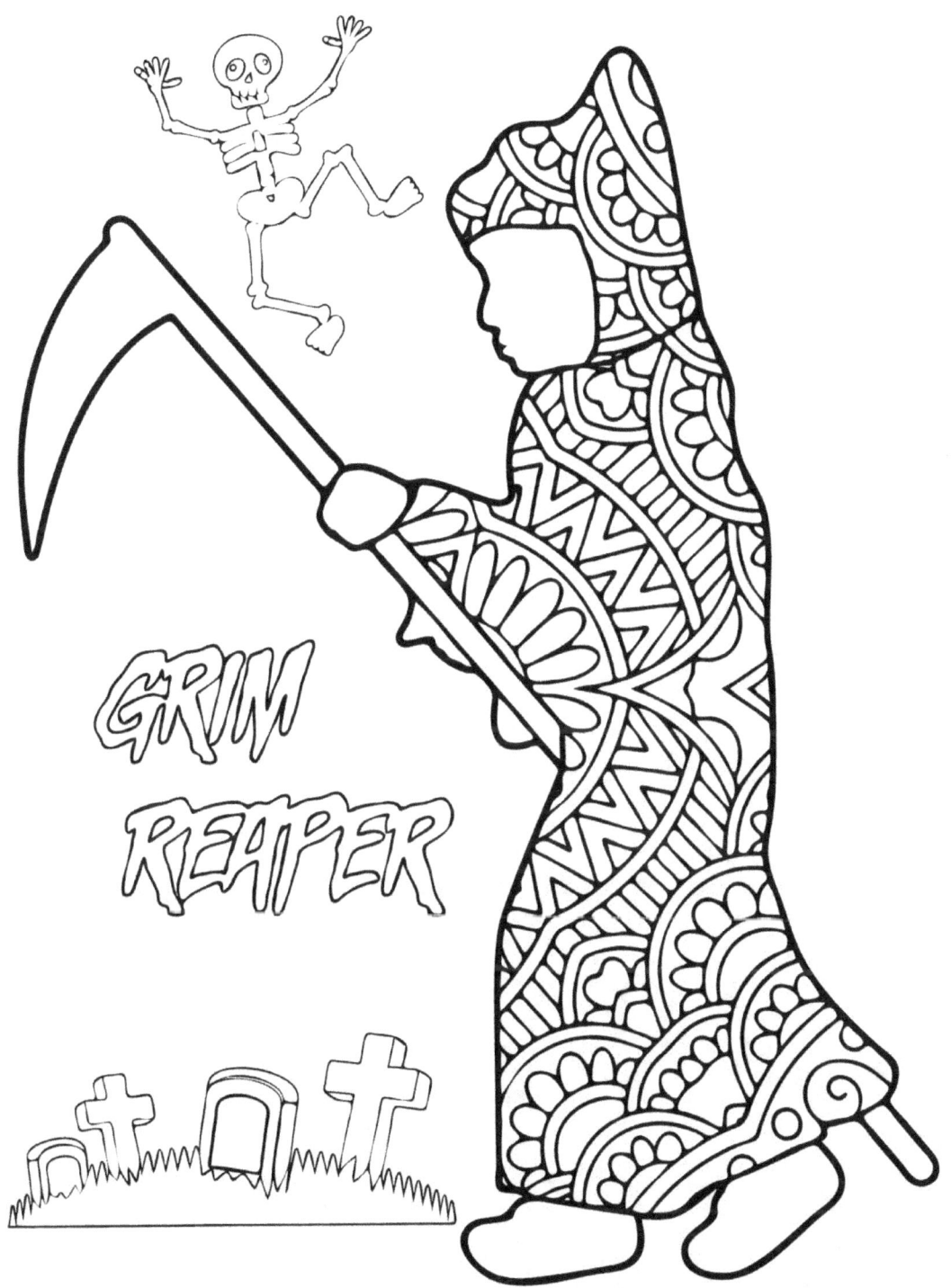

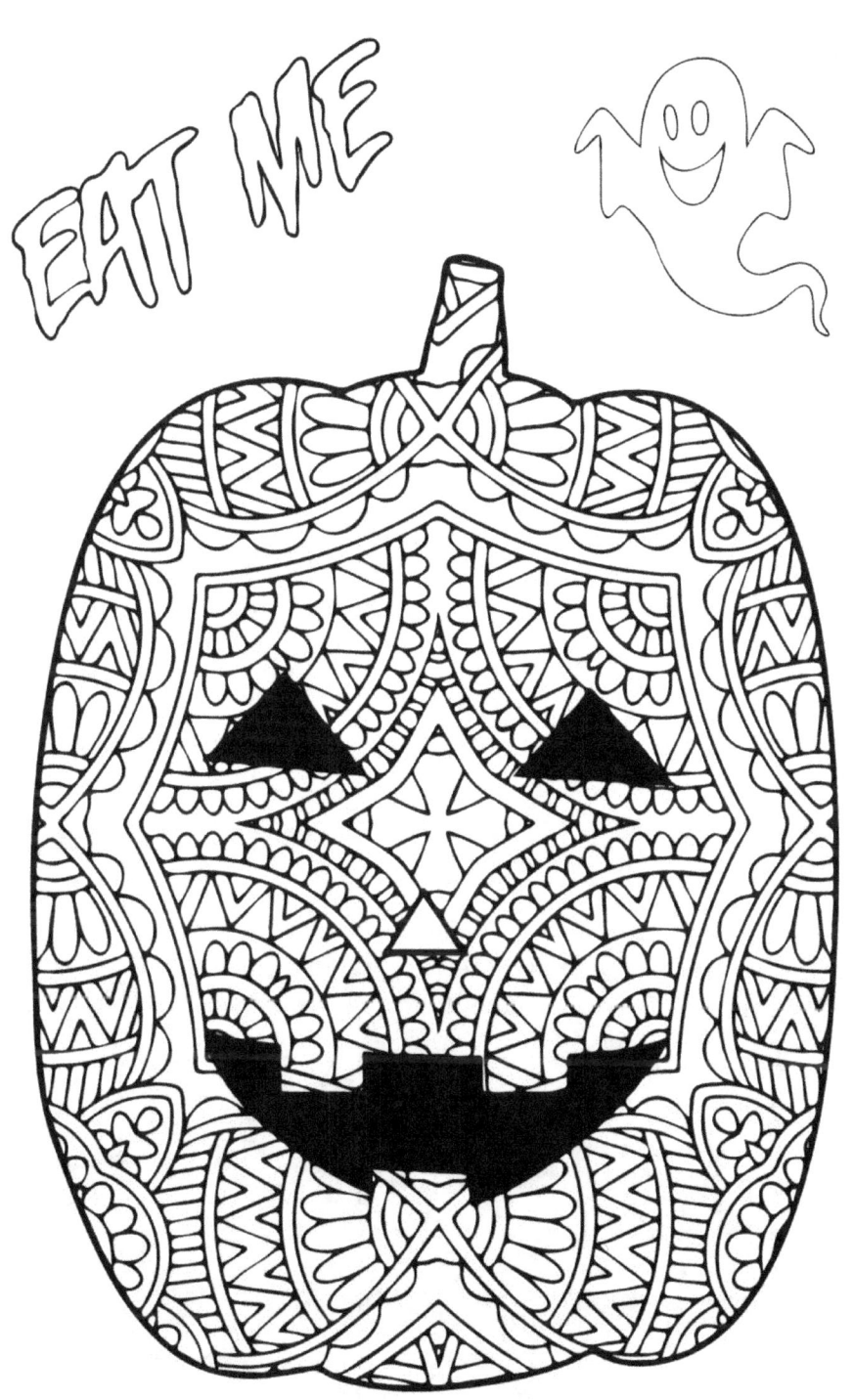

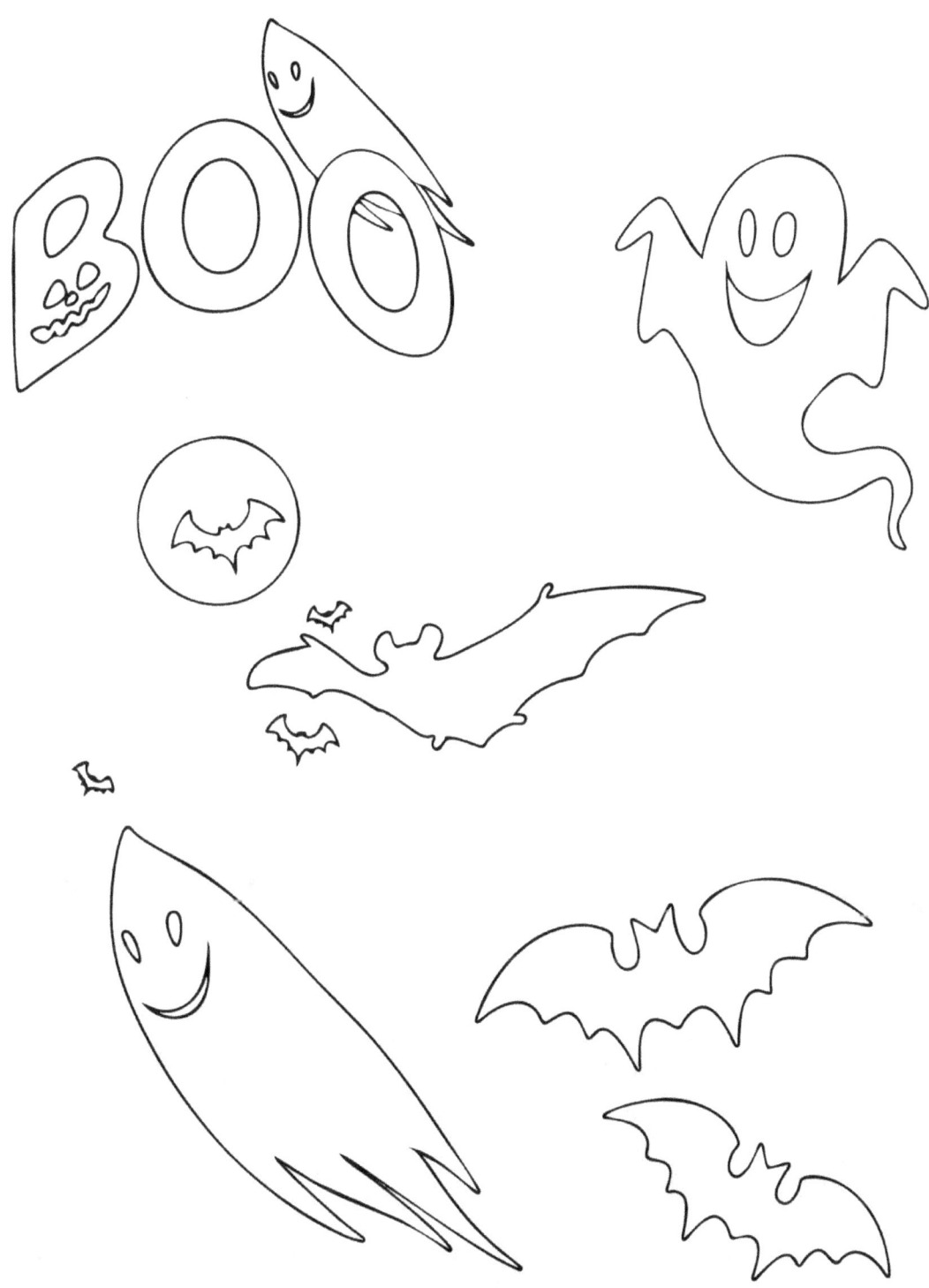

COOL BATS

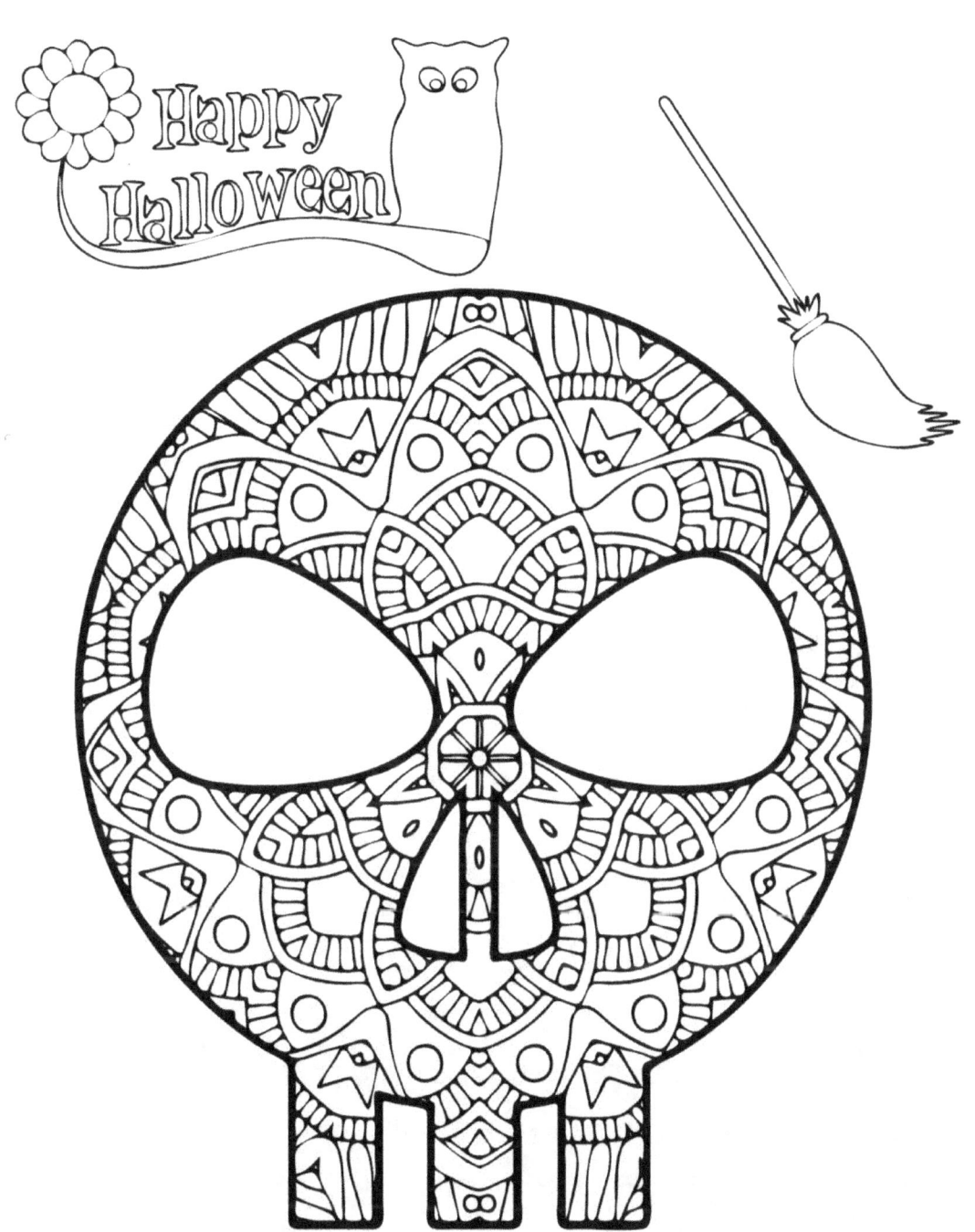

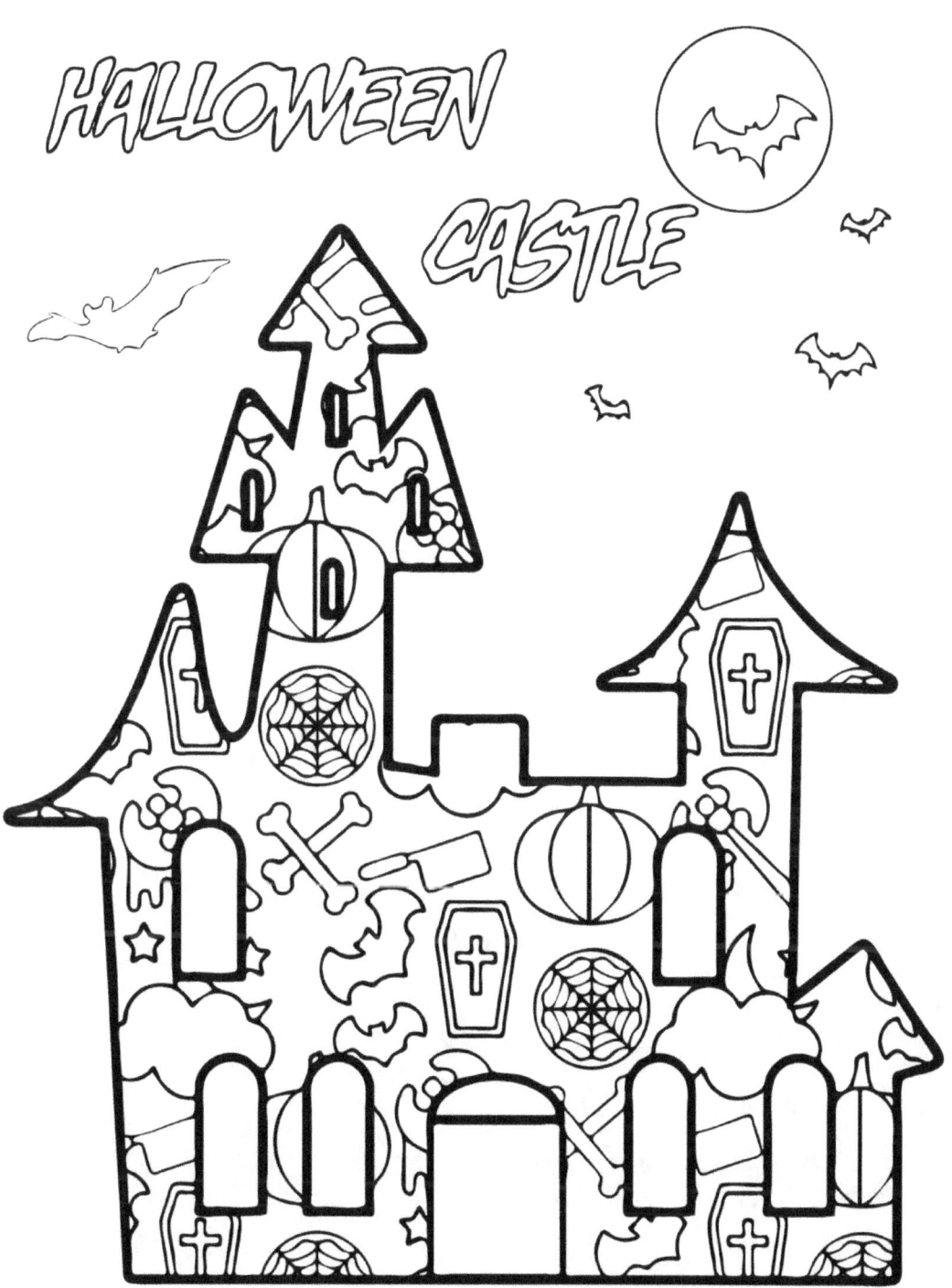

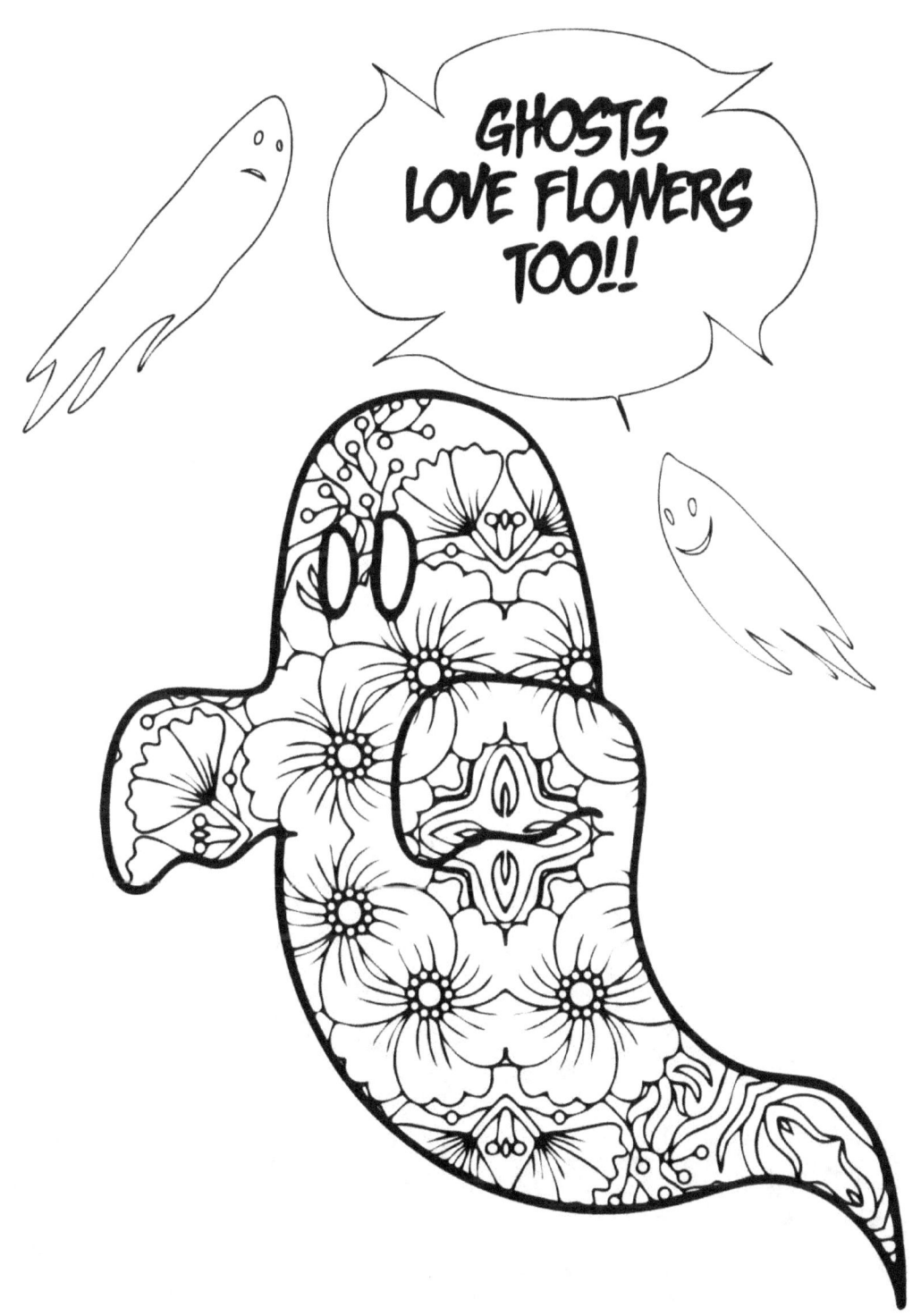

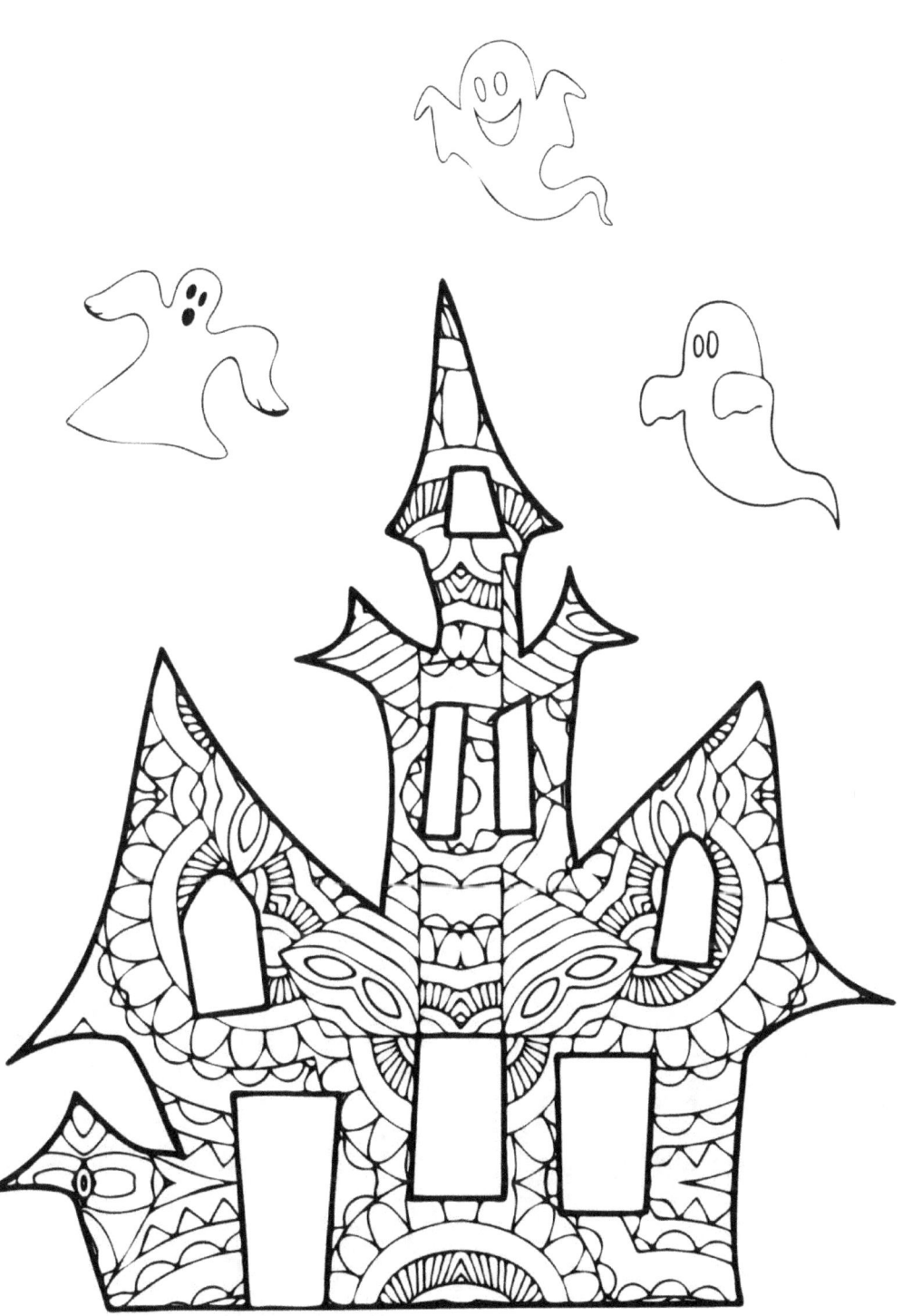

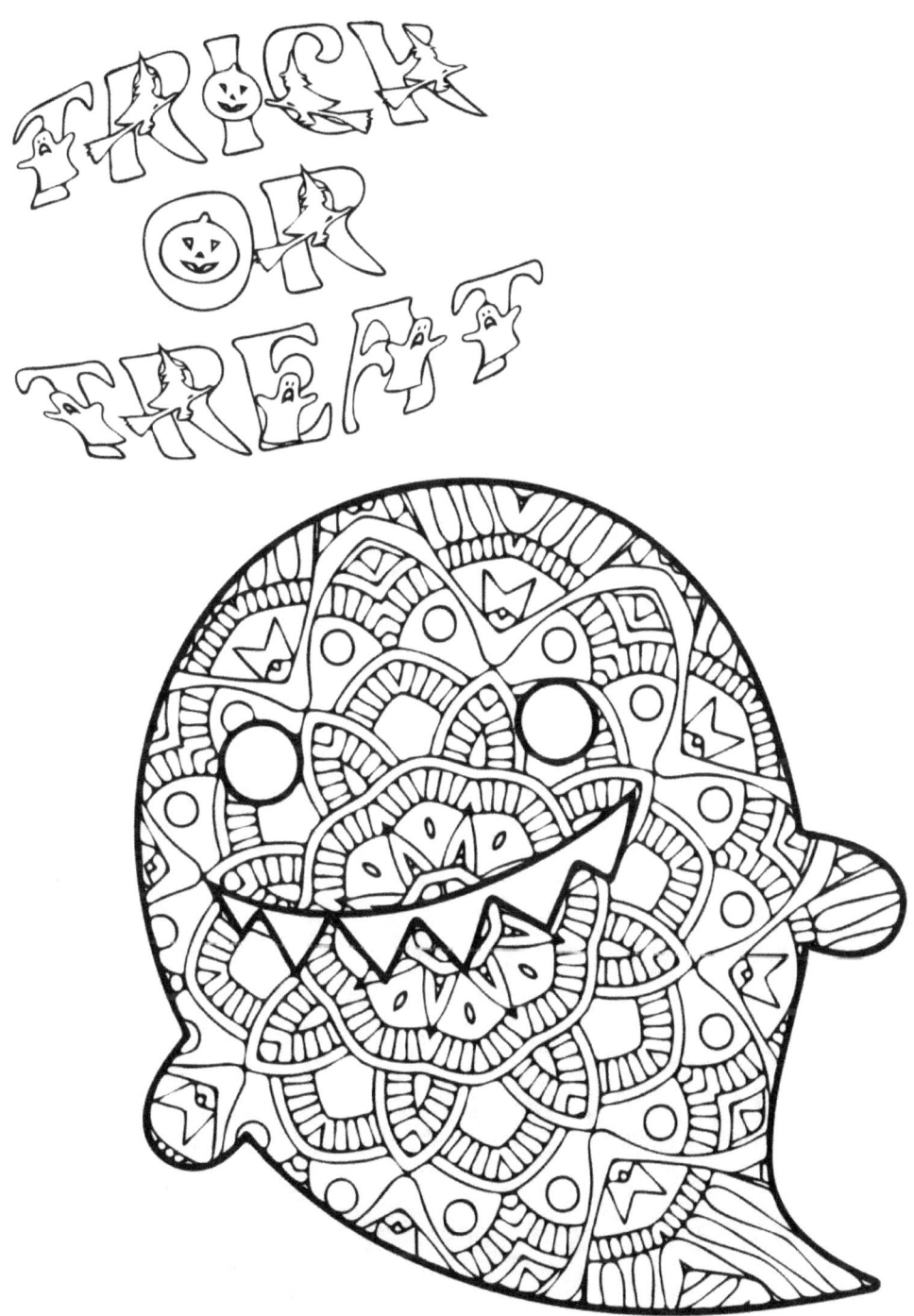

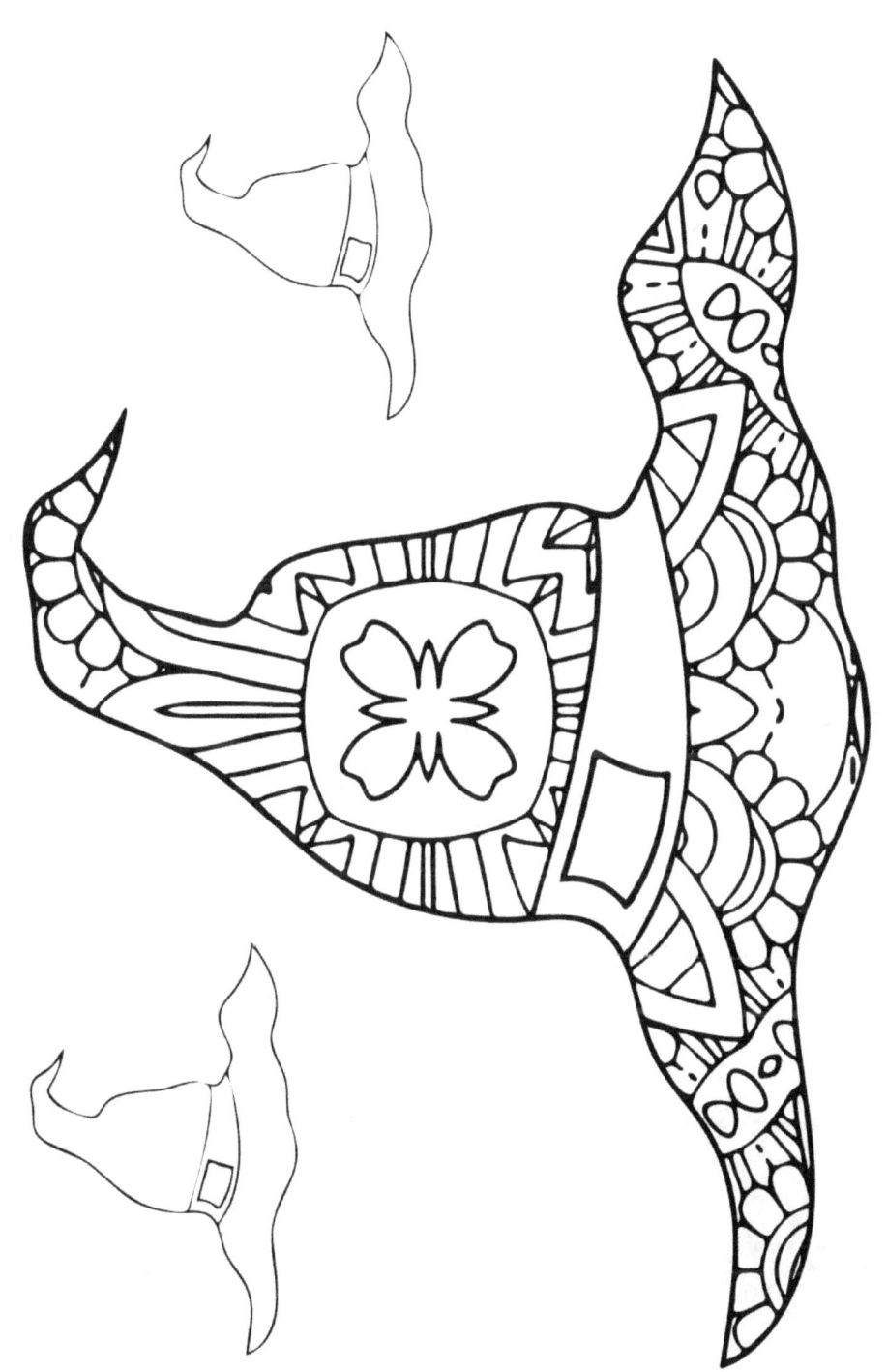

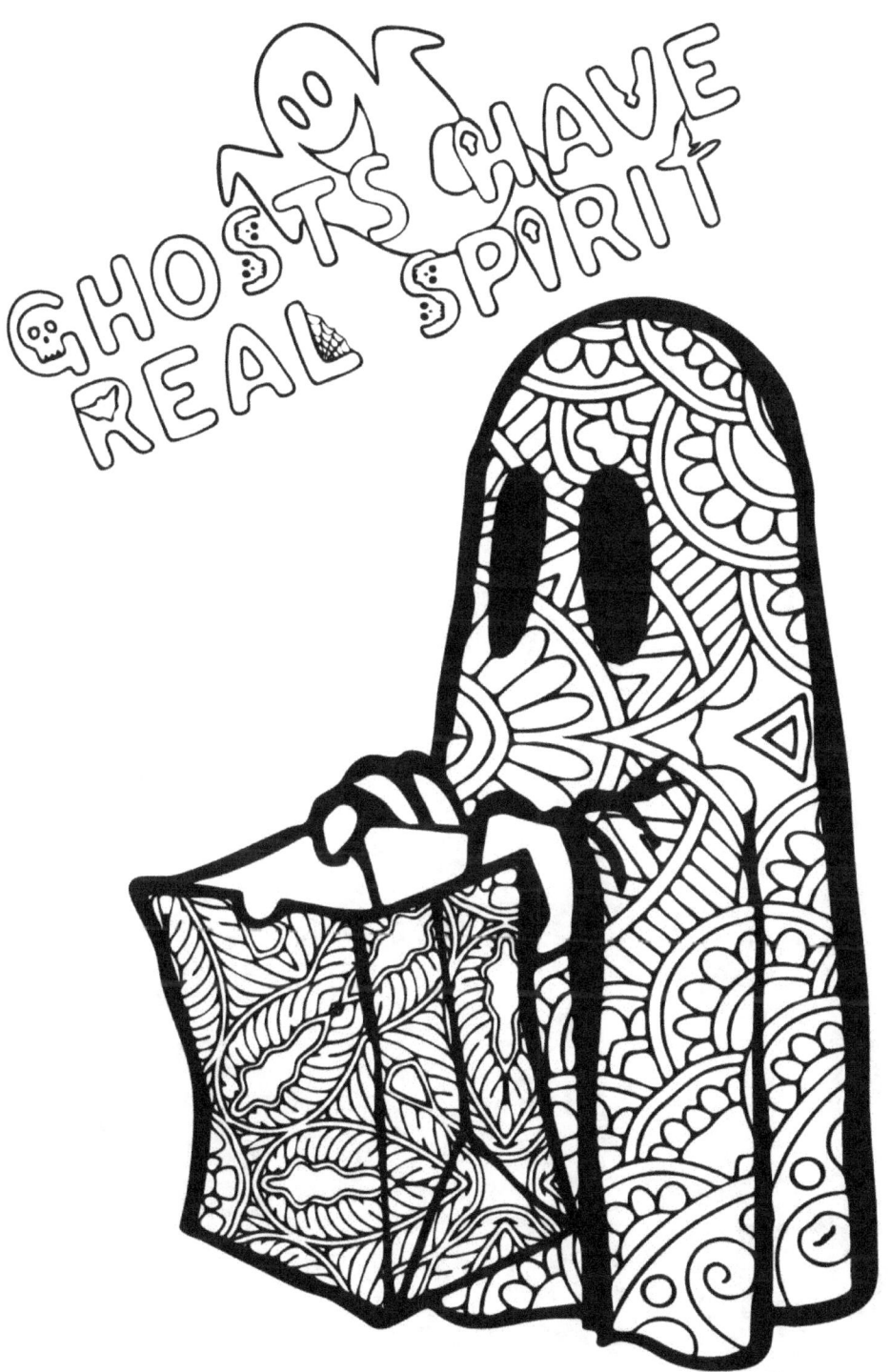

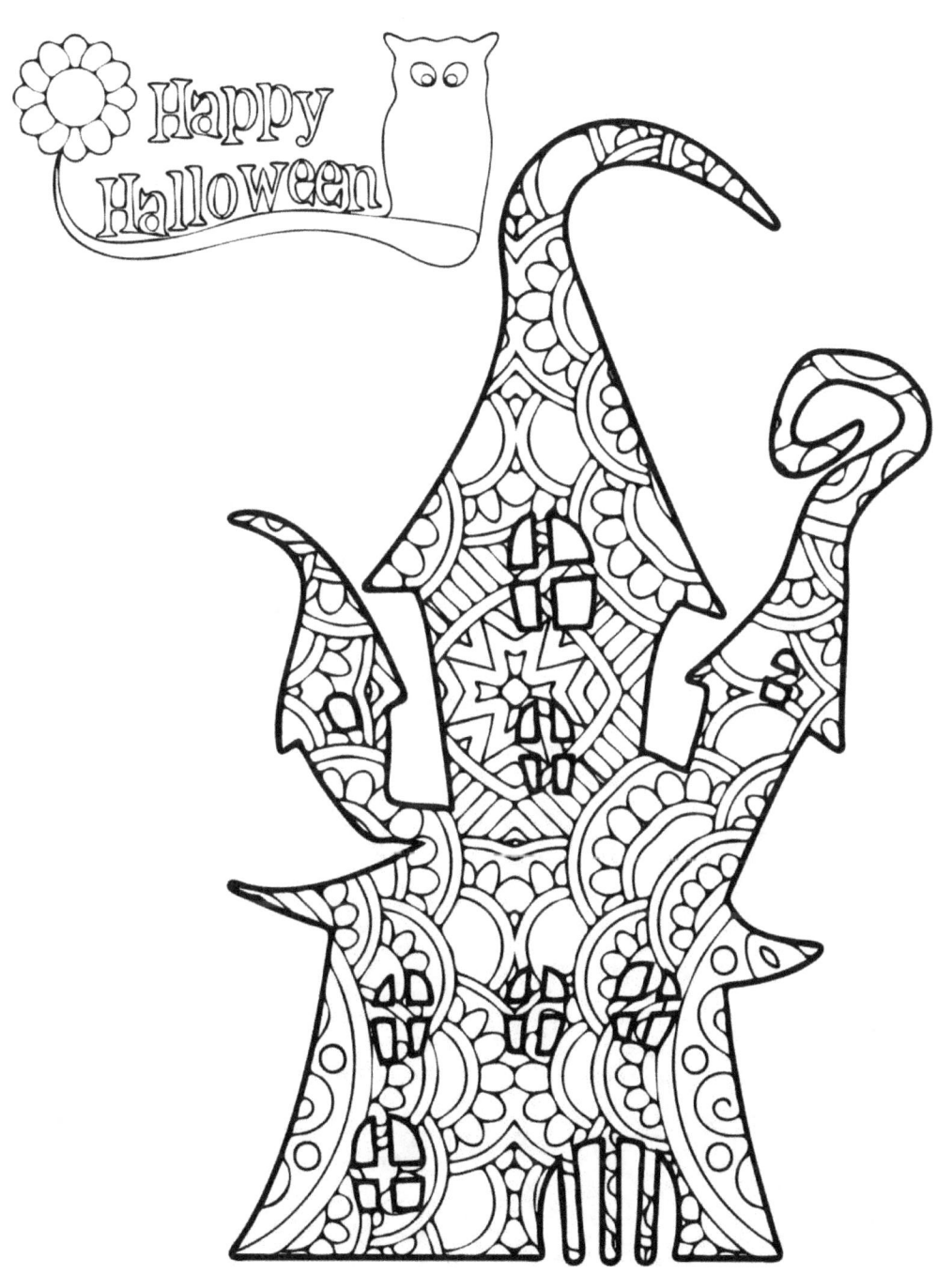

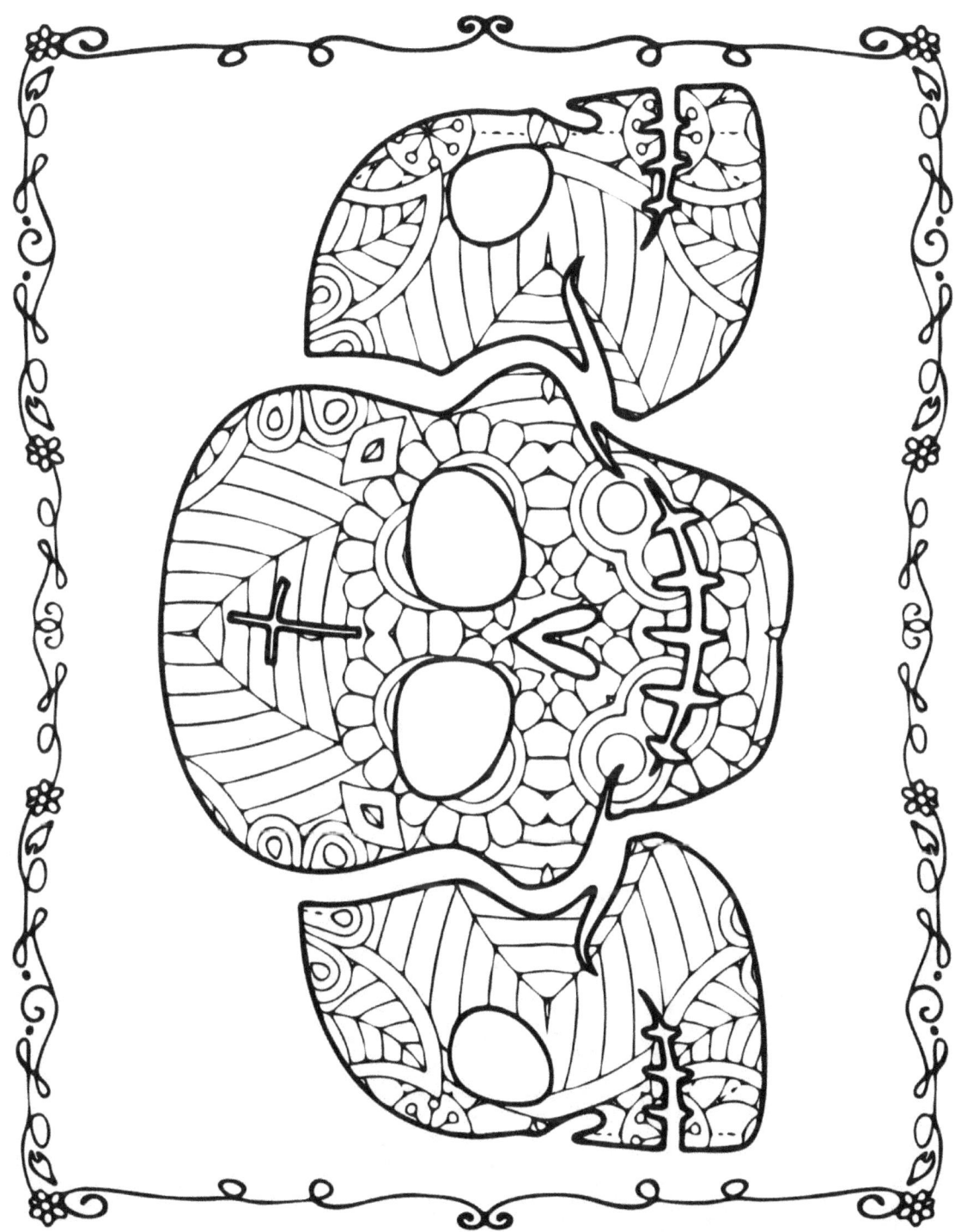

You can use the following samples to practice your palette choices before colouring the main patterns.

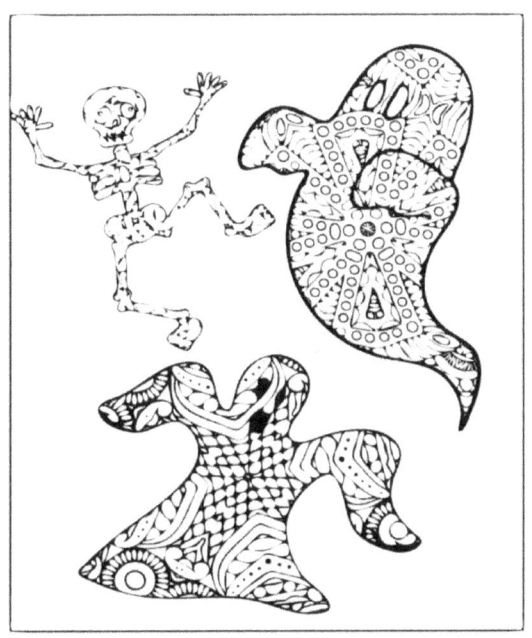
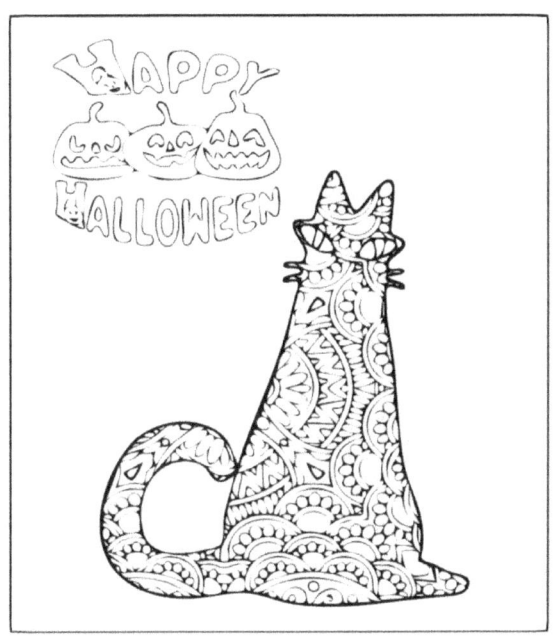
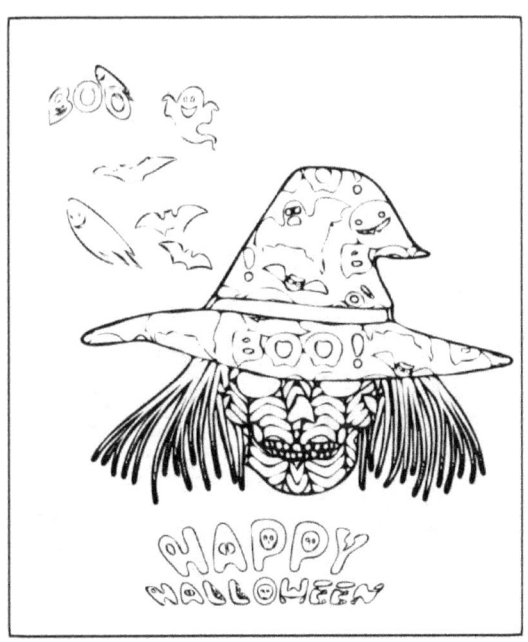
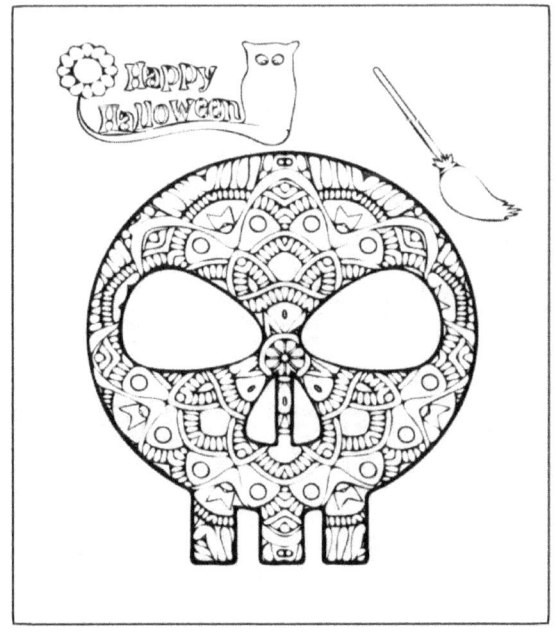

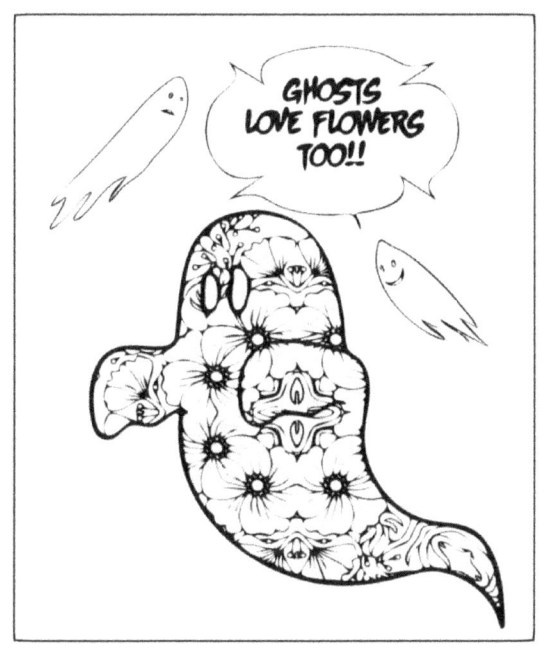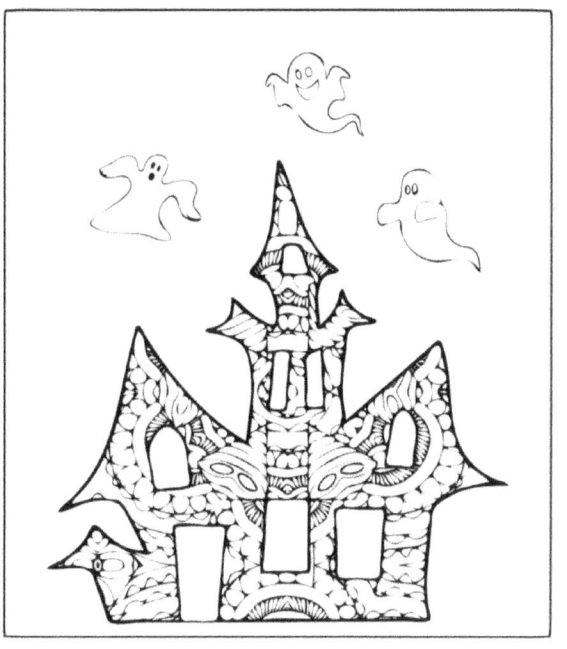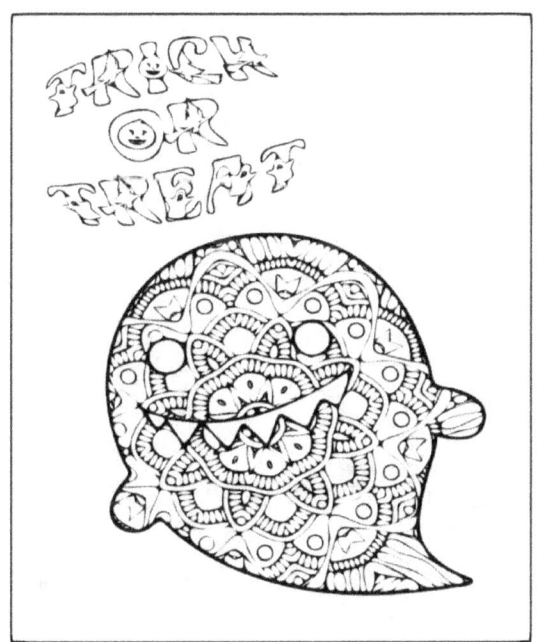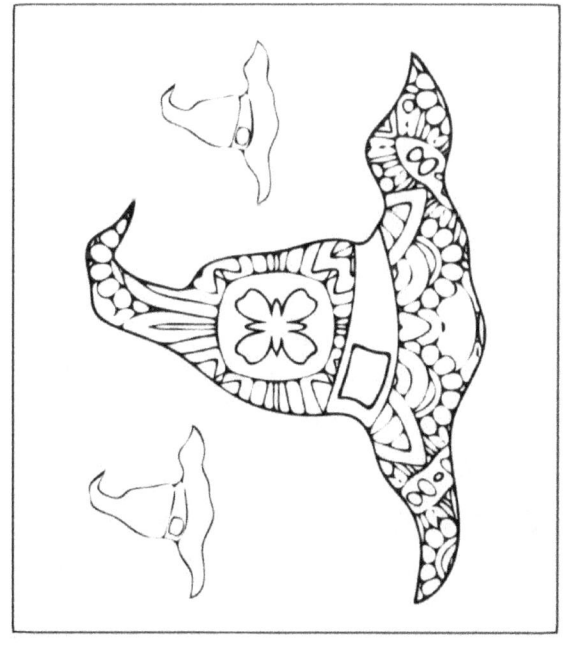

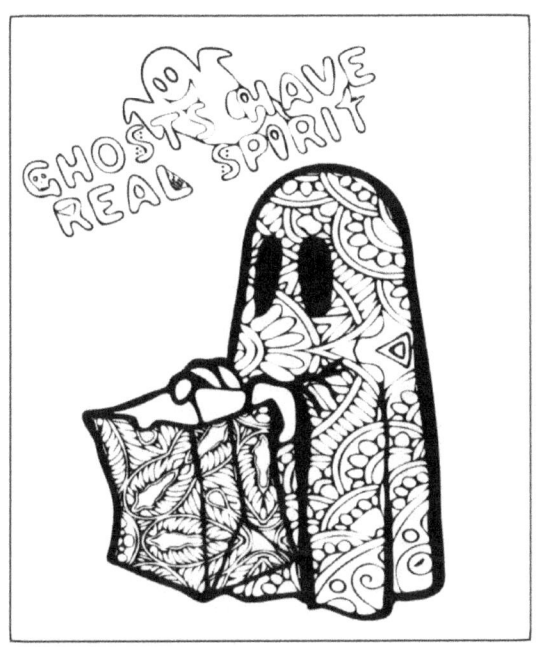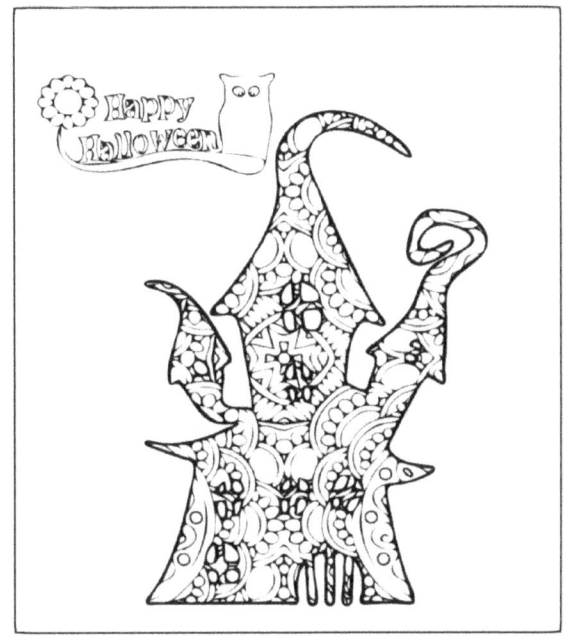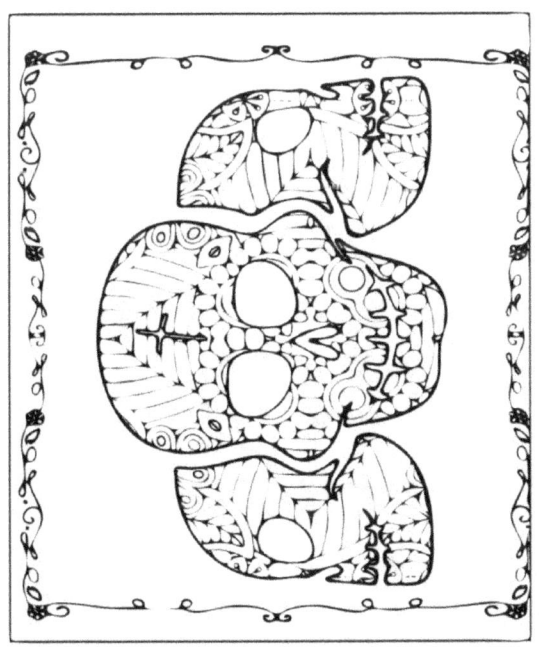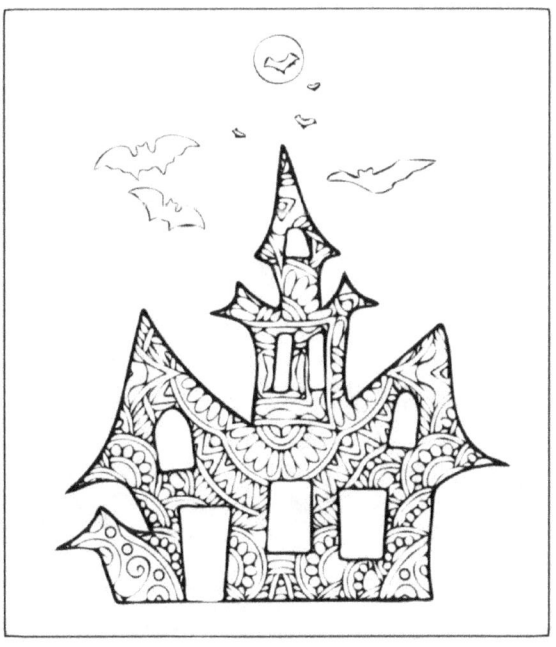

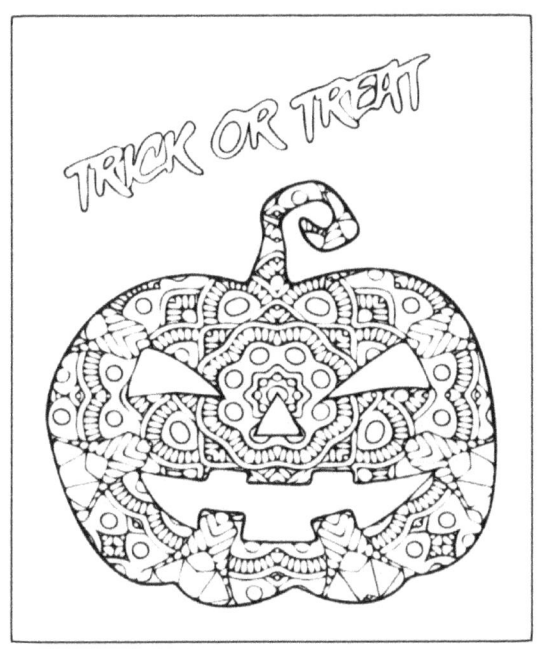
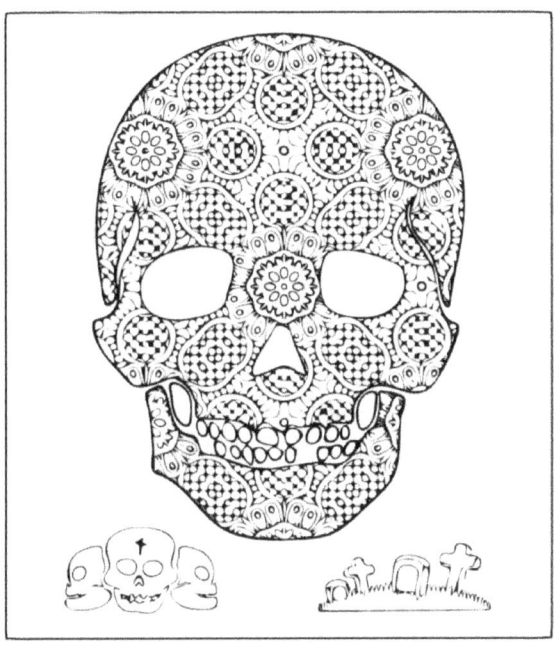
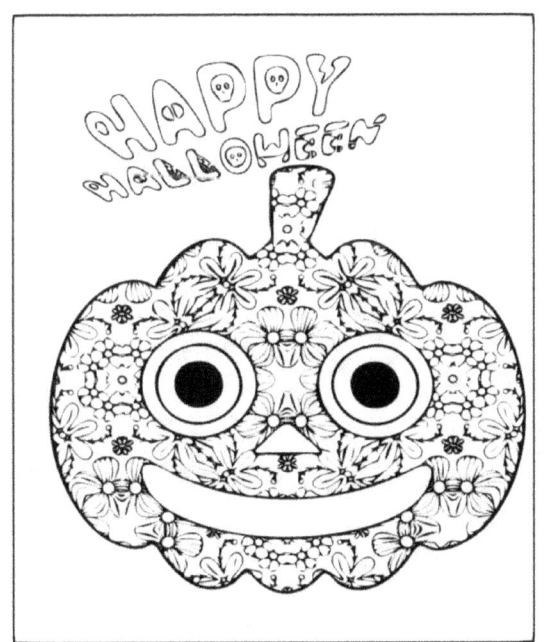
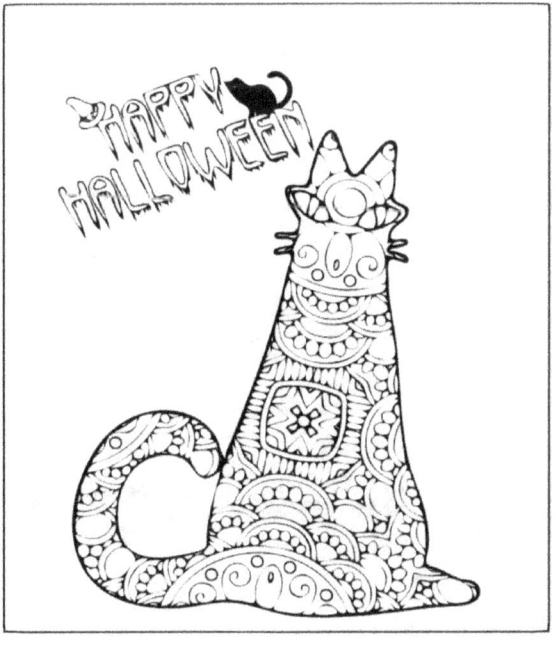

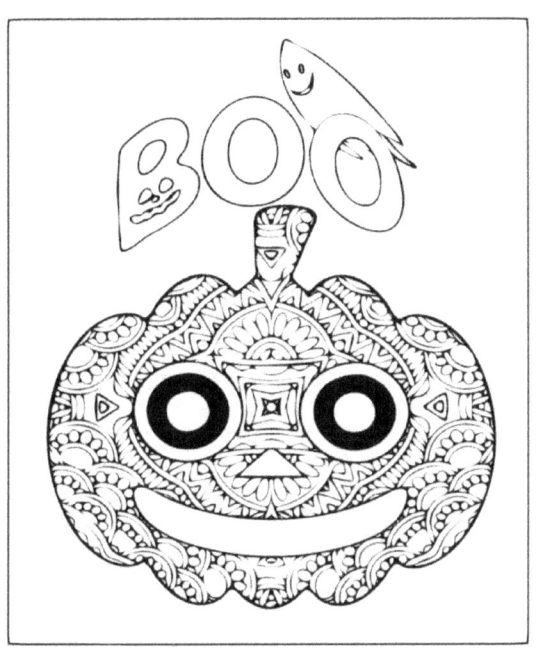
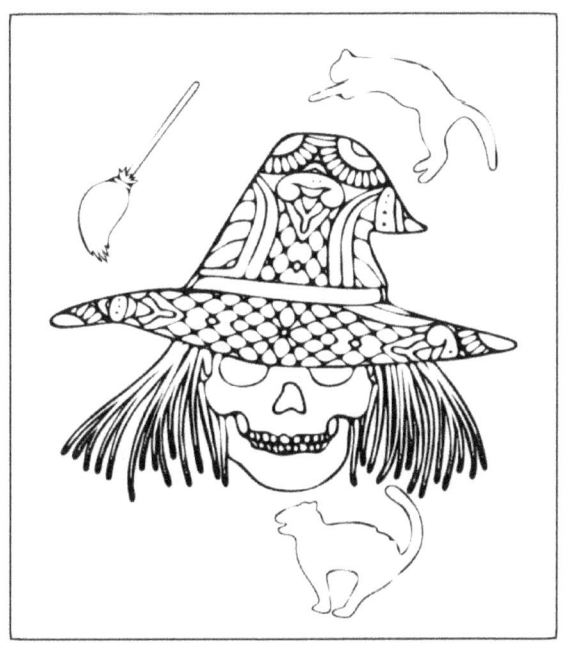
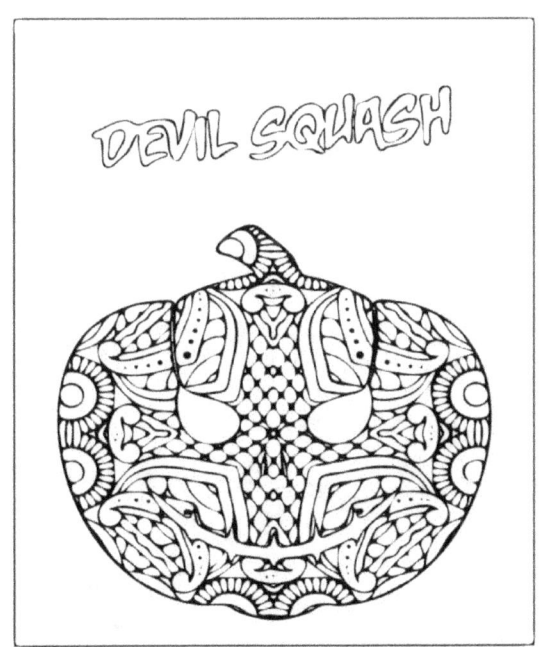
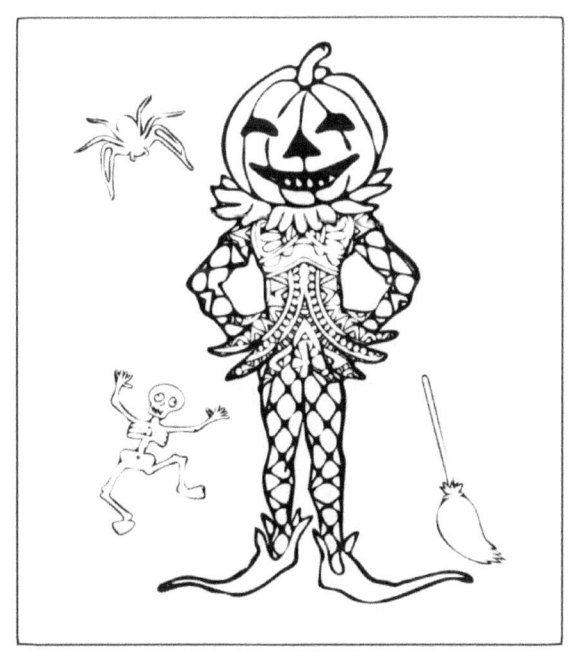

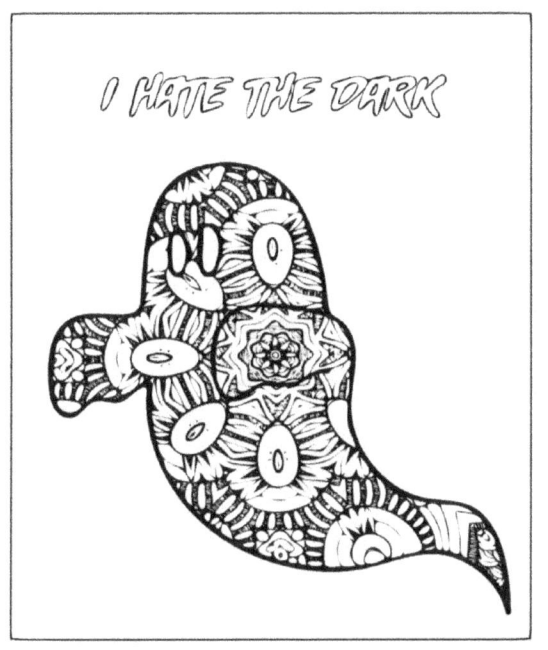
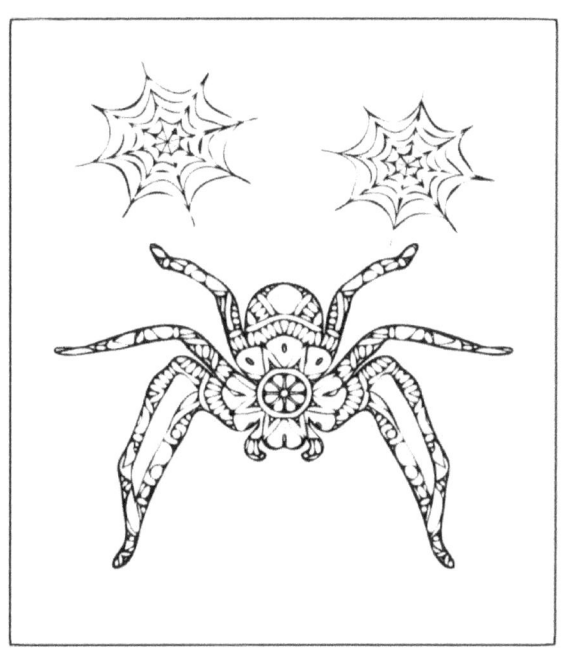
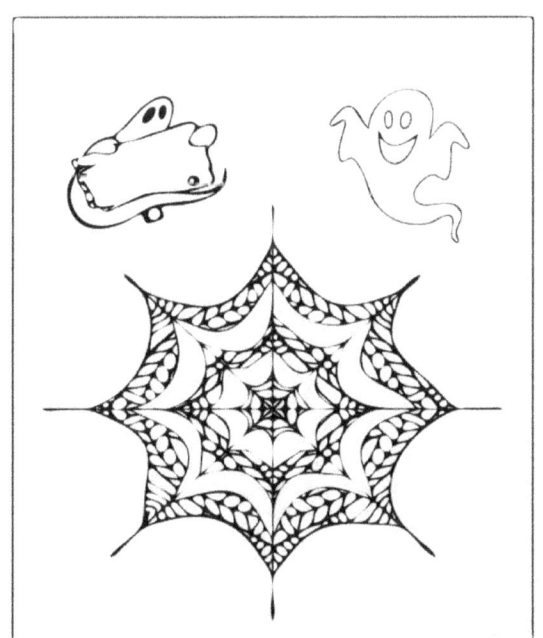
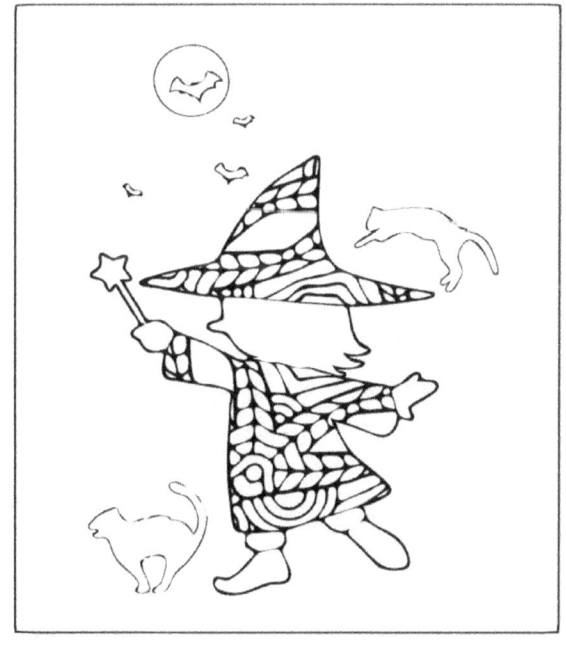

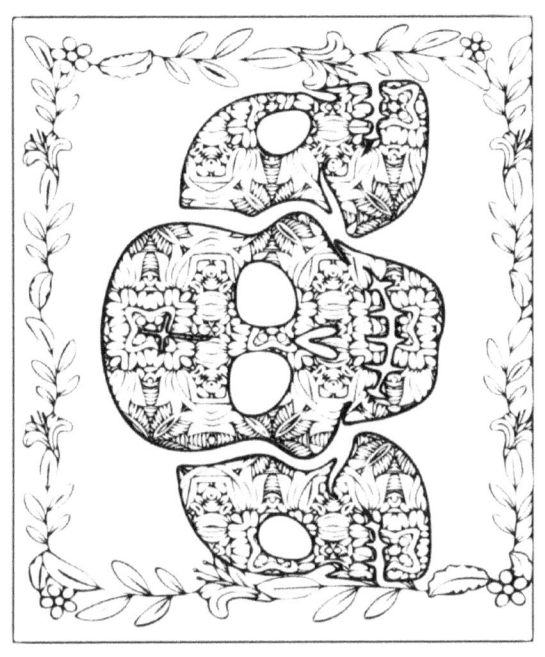
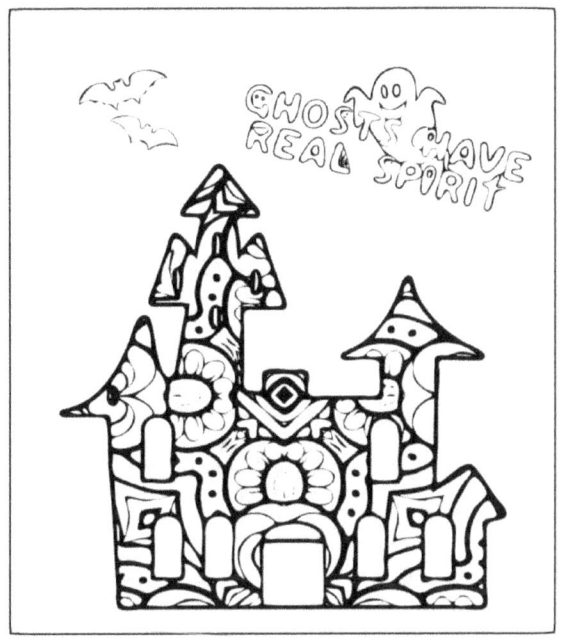
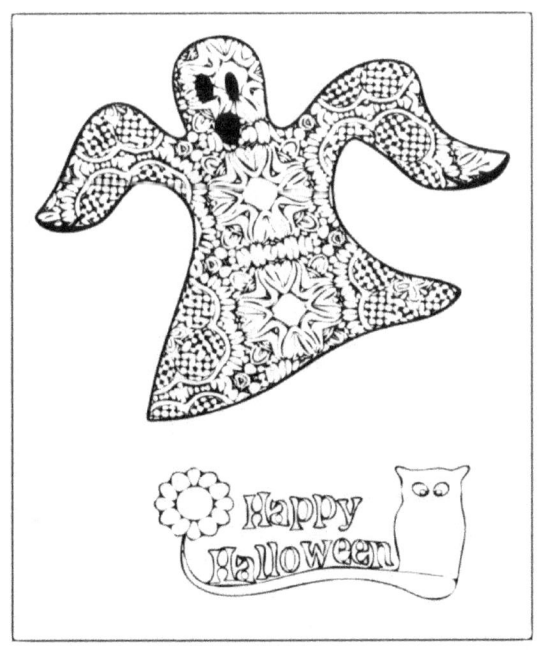
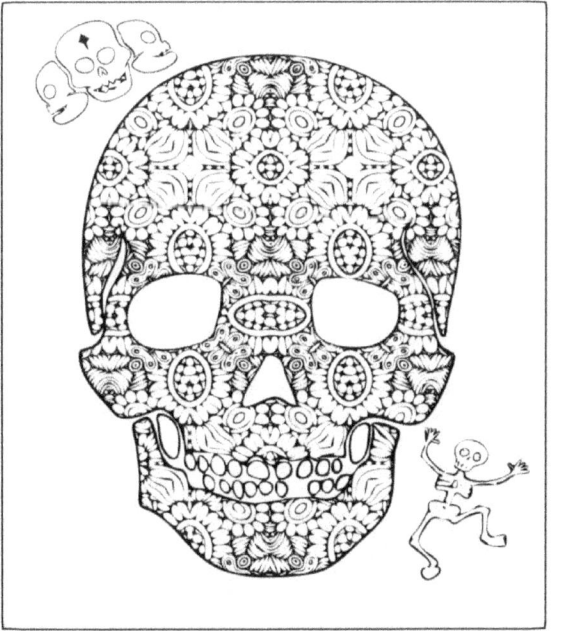

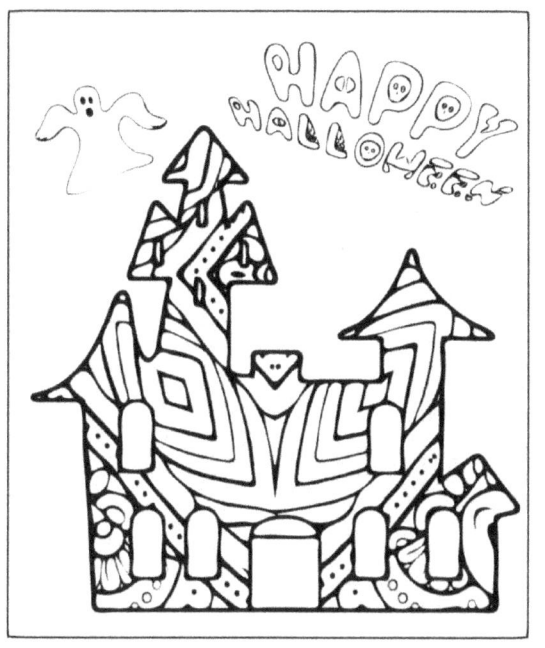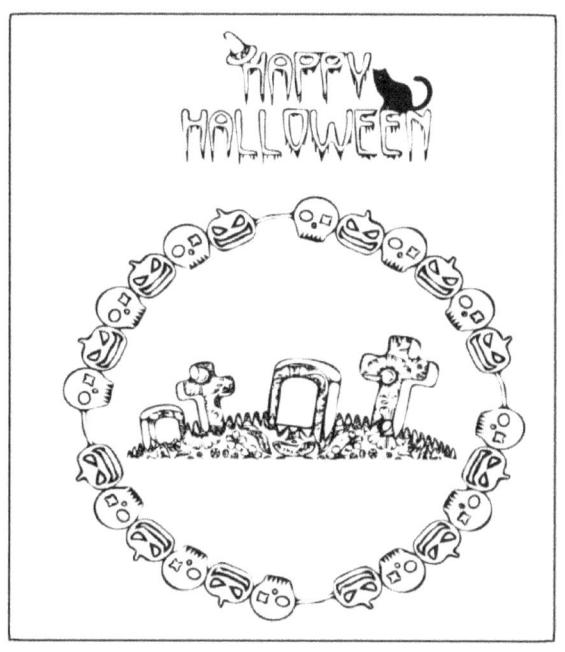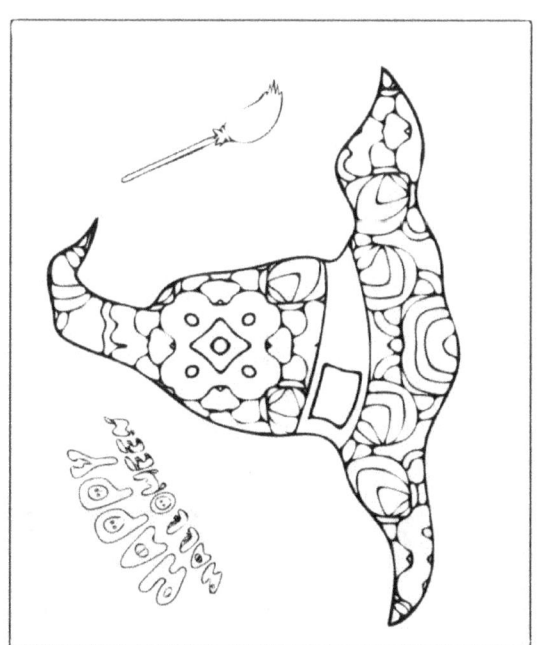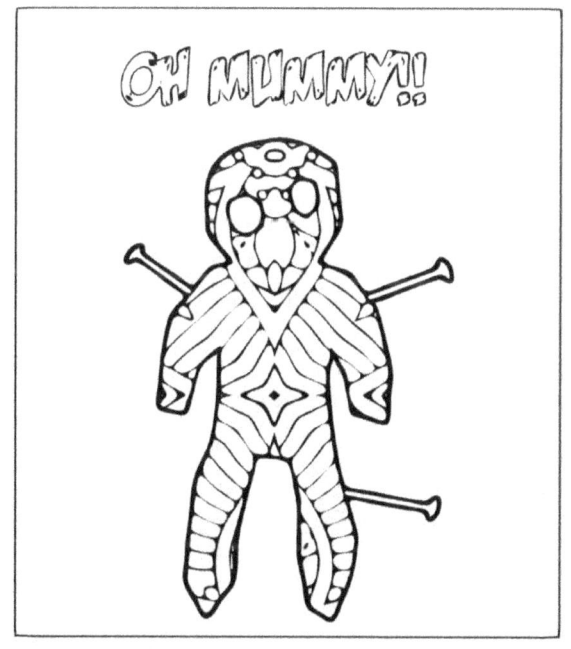

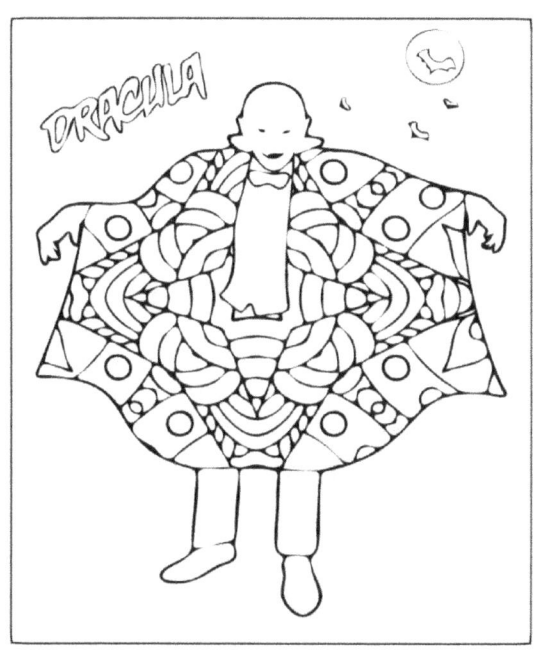
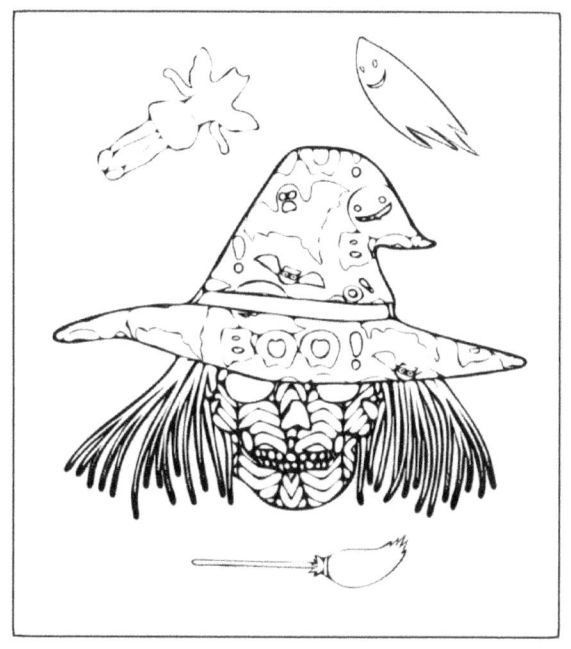
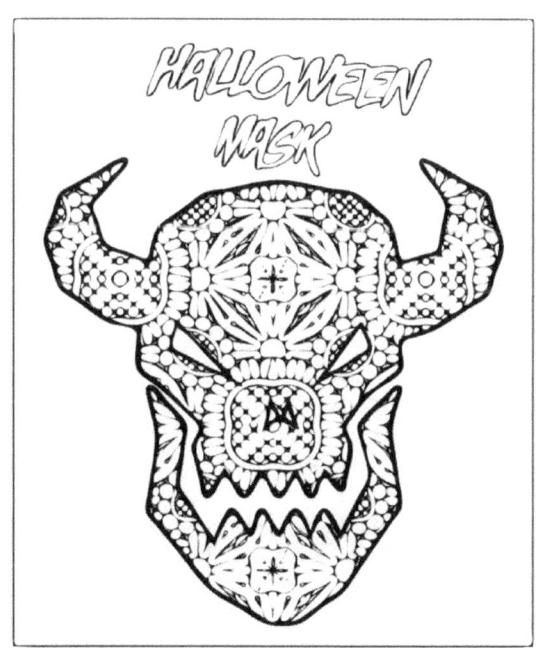
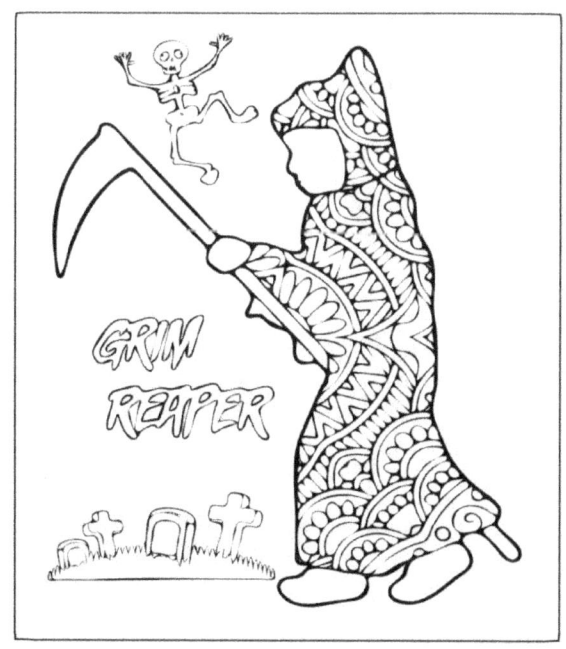

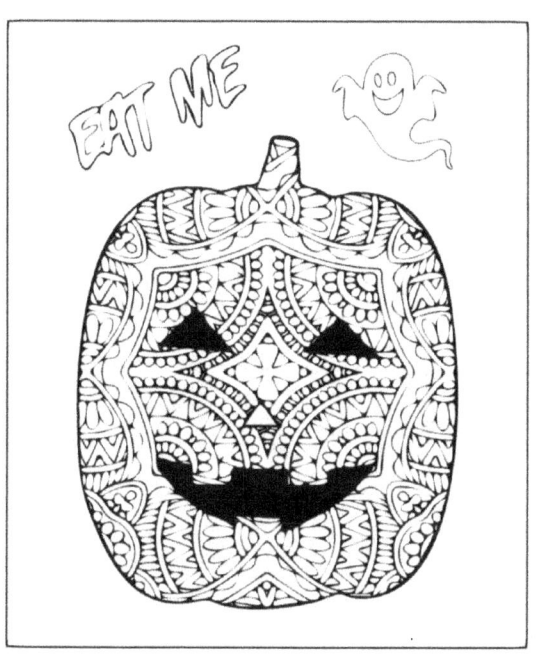
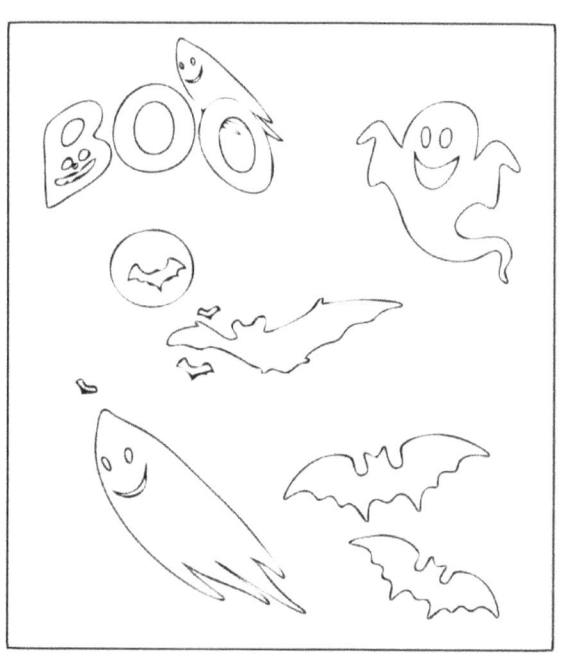
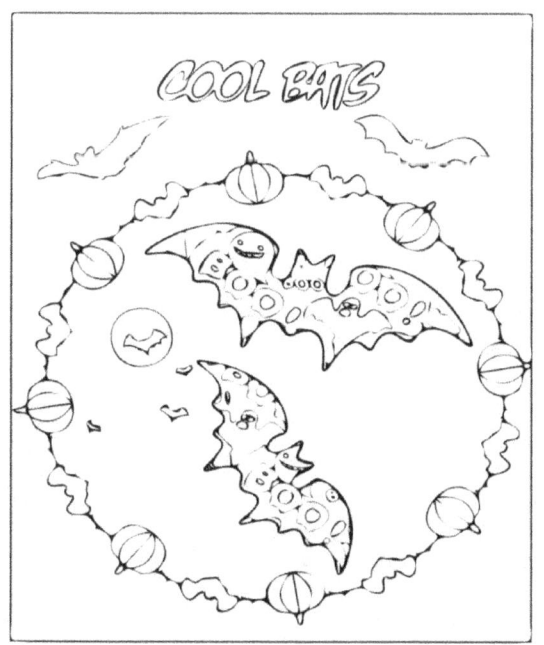
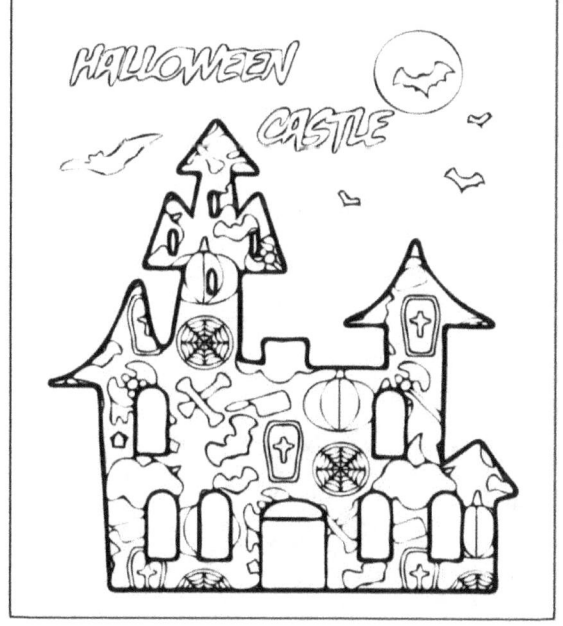

FREE COLOURING BOOK

Grab a FREE colouring book with 30 sample mandalas & patterns taken from the main adult colouring books from Charlotte George

Go to:
www.charlottegeorgecolouring.com

One Last Thing

I hope you have enjoyed colouring the patterns in this book and that you would be kind enough to consider giving an honest review on Amazon.

Also, look out for the other full sized books in my colouring series where there are many more for you to enjoy and all available on Amazon.

Best Wishes
Charlotte

www.ingramcontent.com/pod-product-compliance
Lightning Source LLC
Chambersburg PA
CBHW082342220526
45470CB00008B/2606